Reflections of a Believer

VICTOR EMILIO HADDAD

BALBOA
PRESS
A DIVISION OF HAY HOUSE

Copyright © 2011 Victor Emilio Haddad

All rights reserved. No part of this book may be used or reproduced by any means, graphic, electronic, or mechanical, including photocopying, recording, taping or by any information storage retrieval system without the written permission of the publisher except in the case of brief quotations embodied in critical articles and reviews.

Balboa Press books may be ordered through booksellers or by contacting:

Balboa Press
A Division of Hay House
1663 Liberty Drive
Bloomington, IN 47403
www.balboapress.com
1-(877) 407-4847

Because of the dynamic nature of the Internet, any web addresses or links contained in this book may have changed since publication and may no longer be valid. The views expressed in this work are solely those of the author and do not necessarily reflect the views of the publisher, and the publisher hereby disclaims any responsibility for them.

The author of this book does not dispense medical advice or prescribe the use of any technique as a form of treatment for physical, emotional, or medical problems without the advice of a physician, either directly or indirectly. The intent of the author is only to offer information of a general nature to help you in your quest for emotional and spiritual well-being. In the event you use any of the information in this book for yourself, which is your constitutional right, the author and the publisher assume no responsibility for your actions.

Any people depicted in stock imagery provided by Thinkstock are models, and such images are being used for illustrative purposes only.
Certain stock imagery © Thinkstock.

ISBN: 978-1-4525-3604-0 (e)
ISBN: 978-1-4525-3603-3 (sc)
ISBN: 978-1-4525-3649-1 (hc)

Library of Congress Control Number: 2011910727

Printed in the United States of America

Balboa Press rev. date: 7/11/2011

CONTENTS

Prologue		vii
Introduction		xiii
Chapter 1.	Life. Can it Be a Product of Chance?	1
Chapter 2.	Life After Death?	7
Chapter 3.	Reincarnation?	24
Chapter 4.	From The Universe	39
Chapter 5.	On Birth Control	47
Chapter 6.	A Bit Of History	51
Chapter 7.	A Refreshing Breeze in the Desert	61
Chapter 8.	Study God?	65
Chapter 9.	Can We Understand God's Justice?	68
Chapter 10.	Fragments	75
Chapter 11.	Jesus Christ and His Message	87
Chapter 12.	A Conversation with My Friend Father Juan	103
Conclusion		117

PROLOGUE

And what has become of the history of religion, the ways in which we have known God over generations? At one time God was represented as the absolute King of Kings. He ordered us how to live and we were good, as measured by our obedience toward Him and His word. God would reward us for our unquestioned veneration and punish us when we behaved as unfaithful servants.

All communities had their own religious leaders that spoke in the name of God and knew His will, and the faithful were forced to obey them. God and his human representatives never had to give any explanation for it was enough to decree; and the people followed them.

Later on, almost as soon as their subjects began to question the divine right of the leaders and aspired to be given a voice in their government, they also began to question the divine right of God. The Bible was seen as a document written by men and not dictated by God. Certain laws and customs were interpreted as product of the cultural and economic circumstances of those who established them, not directly from God. Men no longer wanted to be faithful servants, but mature followers of God. When political democracy arose in Europe and America, man started to make his vote count, even in matters of faith and morals.

I have always been fascinated by the impact of the North American environment on Protestant, Catholic, and Jewish traditions that were brought there by European immigrants. The religious authoritarianism had to yield to the North American creed of: this is a free country and no one is going to tell me what to do. The churches that opted for local "democratic" control - Baptist, Congregationalists and Unitarian - established themselves more extensively than those dominated by a centralized hierarchy which had been so powerful in the old country. The North American Catholics felt it in their right to disobey the teachings of their leaders and even so they continued to consider themselves as good and loyal Catholics. The Jews left orthodoxy to one side to follow the voice of reform, or else reacted against the conservatives, demonstrating that a religion is made up of its people and not imposed by a hierarchy. Just as the children that played marbles in the streets of Geneva, religious communities no longer were obedient servants, but were going through an adolescent period of rejection in order to later form a community of mature adults who demanded participation in the establishment of laws that would rule their lives.

The teachings of Piaget deal with not only the mind of a child, but with the future of religion and the search of a transcendental life as well. We learn from him that OBEDIENCE IS NOT THE MAXIMUM RELIGIOUS VIRTUE. A religion whose creed is obedience to its precepts is fitting only for children and the immature and it could have been so for the whole of humanity before civilization evolved. What we read in the Bible: "The Lord hath said" is immaterial, as is the promised reward to a good man and a punishment for a bad one, for it addresses persons in first periods of moral development. The Bible could very well be God's word but is not definitive, for what is limited is not God's capacity to express Himself but man's capacity to understand Him. A religion that insists that to be "good" means to "blindly obey" is a religion that expects us to be children forever.

I have known persons for whom religion was the only guiding force of their lives, and that nevertheless made me doubt that this type of religion was good for them. Some had quite an obsession with sin, an eternal fear of inadvertently violating a precept, of having done something that would offend God and thus lose His love. In others, I noticed an attitude of "now God will see how good and unselfish

I am, and by being so, perhaps get Him to love me". For some Jews, instead of being a serene and spiritually peaceful day, Saturdays become a torment of fear for doing something prohibited. I know Christians who cannot watch a television commercial without becoming obsessed with lecherous thoughts about some of the models, or who believe they have sinned by feeling pride every time someone flatters them for being such good examples to the community. And the spirit that prevails is always "now God will know that I am good, and will therefore love me". I have the impression that all these religious interpretations are incomplete and inhibit a person's development.

A Spanish monk of medieval times wrote in his diary: "I trust in going to heaven after I die because I have never made a decision of my own. I have always followed my superiors' orders so if I have erred, they have sinned, not I."

Along these lines, Erich Fromm, the psychologist, on having emigrated to the United States from Nazi Germany, tried to understand how a cultured country such as Germany allowed a man like Hitler accede to power. In his book "Fear of Freedom", he suggests an explanation. Sometimes, he sustains, life's problems are so overwhelming that we become desperate and believe that there will never be a solution to them. If at that moment someone approaches us and says in a voice that inspires confidence: "Follow me without question, do whatever I ask you to do, and I will get you out of this plight", a lot of us would feel tempted to accept. When life becomes difficult, we yearn to be told: "Don't worry; I'll take care of everything. All I ask of you is your eternal gratitude and obedience".

This desire to transfer problems to another person when life becomes complicated is the child who speaks from within our adult body. When religion fills this need, when religious leaders keep us in a situation of childlike dependence, requiring obedience and demanding our gratitude, they do us little favor. It is precisely because of this that religion failed in Ecclesiastes. True religion should not have to surrender to our complaints. ("This is too difficult.

Tell me what I should do so as to not have to think about it"). On the contrary, it should inspire us to mature, to get rid of childish attitudes. Religion should also encourage us to challenge its own precepts, but not because of an adolescent mood but as informed adults. (*"Encourage"* is an excellent word. Religion should not offer answers but encourage us to find our own.) We should stop treating adults as if they were still children in the name of religion. Ultimately, morals have to go much farther than mere obedience.

Fear of God can really be the beginning of wisdom and the cornerstone of our life, just as the Bible repeats incessantly. But when we speak of "fear of God" we do not mean to fear God. It is not really about "fear" as we know the word today, but respect and veneration. Fear is a negative emotion, oppressive, that moves us to want to flee from what we fear, or even to destroy it. It provokes annoyance toward the person who frightens us and makes us angry with ourselves for being so vulnerable. To obey God through fear is to serve Him with only a part of our being.

On ending his mystic phase, Ecclesiastes could have said to God: "What more do you want from me? I have crawled, offered you absolute obedience, done everything you have asked. Why, then, did you not give me that feeling of fullness, that promise of eternity that I sought?" And perhaps God would have responded: "Do you think that I like to see you crawl? Do you really think that I am so insecure as to need that you lower yourself in order to feel important? Would that man stop quoting the words I delivered to the human race in its childhood and listen to what I attempt to say to it today? From children, and from those that are still spiritually children, I expect compliance, but what you call "absolute obedience" shows that you are incapable of acting as an adult, of taking on the responsibilities of your life. You want to feel fullness and the sensation that at last you have learned to live? Then stop saying: "I did everything you asked me to" and start to say: "You may or may not like it, but I have thought much about it and believe that this is the right way".

True religion should not order us to: Obey! Comply with the law! Live in the past! But should encourage us to grow, be bold, to even make wrong decisions once in a while, to learn from our mistakes. For the faithful, God is not the authority that is constantly indicating what should be done. God is a divine power that drives you to mature, grow, and dare. God does not say, as if to a child: "I am watching you to make sure you do nothing wrong" but rather: "Throw yourself into a world unknown, find your own way, and come what may, I want you to know that I will be with you". As a father who is proud when his children get ahead on their own, God is sensible enough to take pleasure when He sees that we have matured and not when we adopt an attitude of dependence toward Him.

Nor does true religion want obedient persons but honorable ones. What is integrity? The word means wholeness, uprightness, completeness. To live with integrity means to find out that one is, and to always be that person. Religion does not expect us to be perfect. That would not only be impossible and make us inevitably fail, but it would be almost anti-religious as well. If we were perfect, we could never learn, grow, nor change. We would not need faith, and because of our perfection, we would be as great as God. Nonetheless, religion may want us to be complete in another sense: not perfect, but constant. The challenge of a true religion is not that we are perfect but mature, upright at all times, in order to achieve the maximum of our individuality.

Religion is not a scolding father or a school card on which we are graded for our behavior. On the contrary, it is a purifying fire that helps us to free ourselves from all that is foreign to us, all that keeps us from being as we wish to be.

The person God had in mind when He decided that man should evolve as: honest, trustworthy, and sufficiently mature to have overcome his ingenuity without being cynical, a man capable of giving advice for our benefit, not his. That person does not act under fear nor does he wish to cause a good impression but rather acts with profound self assurance of his convictions. He is no saint, nor perfect, but a man who has thrown off all falseness and selfishness until he stands alone with the purest of his complete self, identifying fully with his God.

Throughout my life I have known many persons of integrity that have made a strong impression. They radiate confidence, a feeling of peace obtained when one knows who one is, and what they want. Contrary to those who live in fear of having offended God, a man with integrity lives in accordance with his own high ideals, not for having pleased or offended God. In their presence, one is aware that God has reasons for feeling pleased.

If we are clear about this, we can proceed from the last questions that Ecclesiastes asked to the beginning of the answers he found. Ecclesiastes turned to religion for help in giving him a lasting sense to his life. But since the religion of his time demanded compliance rather than authenticity of self, it could not convert him into a man of integrity. It could have made him "good" in the sense of obedience, but that was not what he sought. He asked something more of God, and since he did not let up in his resolve, he was finally able to find it.[1]

---

[1] KUSHNER, Harold, *Cuando nada te basta*, Emece Editores, S.A., Buenos Aires, Argentina, 1996, pgs. 110-122. I have quoted here fragments from the book. It was selected because I was impressed with the manner in which the author clearly and respectfully expresses ideas with which I am absolutely in agreement and could not myself explain more clearly.

INTRODUCTION

Surely many of you will ask, apparently without an answer: where did life begin? Why and for what purpose do we exist? What is our destiny? What happens when our body dies? Our being will merge into nothingness, converting our passage through life to simply resemble a few guinea pigs in nature's genetic experiment? The most elemental logic convince me that that all this marvelous intelligence in the creation of nature's organisms, that perfection, that balance in the ecological niches, reveals the existence of a supreme Divine intelligence, of an infinite conscience, that has taken charge of the evolution of the species. This miraculous genetic programming, provides the human race with a powerful intelligence capable of discovering many of nature's secrets, create and destroy, with the liberty to choose, every one, his own path in life, every one unique, not equal to another; this separates humanity from all other living organisms, and makes me think that being unique in body we are unique in spirit, and therefore, our spirit must be preserved when our body dies.

We tend to say that we were created in His own image because He has given us an immortal spirit, an intelligence with the capacity to reason and communicate by means of very advanced language, that permits us to reason out complicated matters and, that without Him, we would be limited to the same cognitive level of the apes. We say that God is love, and that He has given us the capacity to love, but the most important similarity, in proportion, is that God as Creator has given us the capacity to create. If we believe that we possess an immortal spirit, then we should be certain that the mind and the spirit transcend to another level of existence once the body has died. Otherwise, He would not have bothered with this only to entertain Himself at our expense. Undoubtedly He has planned something worthy of His greatness and He has reserved new experiences for us, respecting the uniqueness of our mind and our spirit.

But how can we be sure that this is so?

The first option is to have, as many do, a blind faith in what the church tells us, without question.

The second option represents a real quandary, for it introduces us to a labyrinth of speculation. One hopes to be convinced through study, analysis, and common sense. But how to achieve this if we doubt the truth fabricated by men? As we are aware, truth has very questionable concepts which have manipulative overtones, leading to the control of the faithful minds.

I should mention that I have been a practical man, busy with the worries and challenges that life offers.

All went smoothly, in a pleasant, loving, and cordial environment. What more could be desired? But what happens when destiny hits one with a tragedy breaking up the harmony that surrounded one? Doubts about God and His justice.

For me it was what set me off to seek my truth. I had a need to understand the why of this apparent unfairness, and reclaim my vision of a loving God. I wanted to regain faith in Him.

But how?

I spoke with a priest, then another, and others, and what happened? I was even more confused. There was no explanation; the answer was invariably: it is a question of faith, or is a mystery. Seemingly I could find no one to give me an answer that would help.

Throughout a long process – a spark today, a fortunate encounter with an open mind later, a book that was given to me – new ideas awakened in me. A new encounter with someone brighter than myself on the subject, an intuition, and another spark from a universal mind allowed me to get on with my reasoning's.

A slow process, but gratifying, that little by little led me to gather proof of the existence of a spiritual world, and thanks to that, I arrived at the absolute conviction of God's justice, in that death does not exist. This certainty offered me the freedom to live without fear of death, and the assurance that it is a liberation that allows one to pass to other levels of existence. Better? That depends on how you used your free will.

I wish to also make clear in this essay some concepts of the teachings of the clergy on which I differ, always respectful of the basic concepts of our religion – the conviction of a just and kind God, Creator of all things; of Jesus Christ, his son, of the Holy Spirit, and the Virgin Mary – and with no offense meant.

It is true that humanity is plagued with passions, and some have arbitrarily manipulated Christ's message. It is clear that the ecclesiastic hierarchy has lost its way. They call themselves Christians but it is evident that the attitudes of some have shown this to be the contrary. Why? I shall try to explain later on.

Unmistakably, I said 'some', but unfortunately there are many more who submit to this manipulated message in spite of being in disagreement.

It would be unfair not to recognize that kindness, generosity, and helping one's neighbor abound among human beings, within or outside of the church, with or without cassock.

Freedom of expression allows us to voice our opinion on different subject matters according to our own reasoning, whether it is correct or not. It is a right of a thoughtful humanity. The conclusions arrived at in this essay – and I do not refer to the proven historical facts – may be as inaccurate as anyone else's, for who dares to claim that he knows the absolute truth when it cannot be proven? Only God knows.

What is written in this essay is my truth, with all due respect to those who THINK differently.

CHAPTER ONE

LIFE. CAN IT BE A PRODUCT OF CHANCE?

This question is of fundamental importance in that if we are to accept that all this greatness arises through random combinations, then religion must be eliminated because we would, at the same time, be denying the possibility of the existence of a creative intelligence, which converts the concept of life after death of the body into an utopia, the possibility of miracles, and of the existence of other levels of life. To arrive at this conclusion, as I see it, is inacceptable, since it is evident that in recognizing a manifest intelligence in creation, it completely defeats the concept that all that greatness is an accidental product of random combinations of molecules. We should persuade ourselves that creation is CAUSAL and actually it is not so difficult to eliminate the possibility of a random, casual creation.

It is evident to me that in order for molecules to organize in an orderly and appropriate manner to create life, which is so inconceivably complex and perfect, the intervention of a higher intelligence is required. An intelligence that exceeds all possibilities of humanity's marvelous but limited intelligence. All of its magnitude. An intelligence that modifies the genetic design of organisms, as the surrounding environment changes. Finally, after thousands of millions of years, the environment is ripe to sustain life of organisms like you and me, a real miracle that allows us to be aware of ourselves and our surroundings, able to analyze, project, communicate through language, discuss ideas, institute laws, express our feelings, create, and unfortunately, also destroy. All this and more, much more, thanks to the intelligent design of the Creator.

There are those who believe that all this wonder is a product of the random combination of molecules that through trial and error, little by little, reaches the right combination and thus, eventually, leads to the correct sequence of a perfect organism. I respect their opinion, but differ totally. If coincidence were to achieve that incredible task, then we should accept that coincidence is intelligent, and therefore a creating intelligence. One way or the other, we would inevitably be proving the existence of a superior intelligence. But to be able to speak of intelligence, we should accept that it is obvious that it too should be capable of planning, analyzing, and programming for which the concept of creation by coincidence CANNOT BE INTELLIGENT, for IT IS INCAPABLE OF THINKING IN AN ORDERLY MANNER and therefore NOTHING can be created from it. The organisms should emerge perfect, complete, through a marvelous genetic programming. Without this process, which is inexplicable to us, no complete organism could exist.

In my search, I became convinced of the necessary existence of an intelligence - which I may call divine – exceeding all comprehension, and what we call God, omnipotent, omnipresent, of pure spirit, organizes the chaos with His LAWS, and manifests Himself in all the marvels of creation. Thus, it is logical to think that He decides to respect His laws because they are perfect.

Evolution has followed an orderly sequence through thousands of millions of years. Organisms emerge perfectly, by means of a marvelous genetic programming from one stroke, not through random changes or piecemeal. It is clear that life arises from the simplest of microorganisms and develops little by little in an orderly, perfect fashion. As such, it progresses from simplicity to complexity, seeking the esthetic, until it reaches the creation of intelligent beings capable of awareness of the Creator's work. If God could create everything perfectly from the beginning in a magical gesture, He would not have bothered to do so through programmed evolution over thousands of millions of years. It is clear that it is illogical to believe that the Almighty can, with one magical touch, bring trillions of bodies back to life, each one with different characteristics, none the same, for it would violate the universal laws that He Himself legislated. To me, it is clear that God is no magician. He performs his work in accordance with His laws and His science.

You may ask: thousands of millions of years? That is an absurdly long time.

For humanity, who lives in a four-dimensional sphere, it is indeed inconceivably eternal, but we must remember that time does not exist as such in other dimensions of existence. Time is relative, as it is in the world of matter, since it depends on the perception of the individual; for example, as when for someone at a party who has had a few drinks, five hours would seem all too short, whereas for a person that is in great pain, those same five hours would appear eternal.

Albert Einstein, in his brilliant hypothesis of the theory of relativity, predicted, as it has been demonstrated, that time passes much more slowly for someone who travels at a good speed, and faster for someone who remains stationary. Of course in that case, there is little speed, and the difference is minimal, but when we speak of speeds closer to that of light, an hour for the traveler in time can equal many, many days for those that remained on earth.

I wonder: what is the speed limit for the spirit? That of light or that of thought? How are we to know? But on not being limited by a slow body, nor subject to the force of gravity, takes on another dimension outside of the limitations of time space, which is another dimension governed by different laws of physics, it is possible that any one of the two options should be within reach. Thus, for a spirit, time can no longer be measured, for it passes by differently, according to the speed with which it is possible to go from one place to another.

REFLECTIONS OF A BELIEVER

The following is a quotation from *A short history of nearly everything (2003),* author, Bill Bryson.

Proteins are obtained when you unite amino acids, and we need a great deal of them. Nobody really knows, but there can be up to a million types of proteins in the human body and each one of them is a miracle. According to the laws of probability, proteins should not exist. To make one, you need to group together the amino acids - the bricks of life - in a set order, similar to how letters are grouped together to compose a word. The problem is that the alphabet of the amino acids is generally extraordinarily long. To write collagen, the name of a common type of protein, you need to write eight letters in correct order. To create collagen, 1055 amino acids must be placed exactly in correct sequence. The possibilities of one molecule of 1055 amino acids, such as collagen, self-organizing in a spontaneous manner are clearly null. It just will not happen. That certain random events would actually produce a protein would result in something of an amazing impossibility, comparable to a whirlwind passing through a junk yard and leaving in its wake a fully assembled jumbo reactor - a colorful metaphor made by the astrologist Fred Hoyle.

Nevertheless, we are speaking of hundreds of thousands of proteins, perhaps a million, each one unique and vital; for what we know each one to keep you in good health. And there it all starts. In order for one protein to be useful, it must not only group together amino acids in proper order, it must convert itself into a kind of chemical origami and assume a specific form. Also, after having reached that structural complexity, a protein will serve you no purpose if it cannot reproduce itself, and proteins cannot do that. For that they need DNA. DNA is a whiz at reproduction; it can make a copy of itself in seconds, but is incapable of almost anything else. Thus, we find ourselves in a paradoxical situation. Proteins cannot exist without DNA and DNA is worthless without proteins. Are we to suppose, then, that they emerged simultaneously with the purpose of helping each other? If that were so: poof! And all that, without **RNA,** is worthless.

REFLECTIONS OF A BELIEVER

And yet there is more. DNA, proteins and the other elements of life could not prosper without some type of membrane for support. Neither atom nor molecule has ever reached an independent life. If you were to detach an atom from your body, it would be as alive as a grain of sand. These various materials can only partake of the amazing dance of life when joined in the nourishing refuge of a cell. Without the cell, they are mere interesting chemical substances. But without chemical substances, the cell also lacks purpose. If each needs the other, how could the community of molecules first arise? It is not unusual to call this the miracle of life. Nor is it unusual that we are just beginning to understand it. End of Bill Bryson's quote.

I should add that the membrane of itself is a marvel, for it not only contains the cellular elements but it would serve no purpose otherwise. It is endowed with countless specific receptors which let in only those elements required by the cell in order to function, rejecting those that are not needed. This membrane is a true engineering electro-chemical design wonder, an amazing proof of creative intelligence. Let us not forget, too, that the cell could not function without the help of symbiotic bacteria's, the famous mitochondria's, that operate with DNA and RNA independently of the nucleus of the cell, and that they are charged with producing the energy for the cell to carry out its functions. And the bacteria's that help in the digestion of food? And the vitamins necessary to the health and workings of the organism? Without all this, and more, we would not exist. If upon considering a cell, we are faced with the impossibility of its arising by chance, what may we say of that enormous amount of different cells, each one specialized in a particular function in the creation of an organism, all essential, and marvelously programmed in one genetic stroke.

If an in-depth analysis of the development of a baby from the moment a sperm fertilizes an ovum, up to the birth of a human being, is made, it would reveal this to be an astounding miracle, an amazing intelligence present in a microscopic package of chromosomes in which the information to carry out the proper sequence has been written of when and how the different types of cells, already specialized, should intervene to construct that marvelous organic machine, all at the right moment, including instructions for all the characteristics of the organs to be developed, perfect in their construction and workings, and each and every one of them a wonder of design, science, and intelligence. It is here that the absolute existence of a creative intelligence is revealed to me, humbling me, while at the same time filling me with joy, for I am convinced that God does exist, and therefore feel sure that our passage in this life is owing to a divine plan, where the existence of our being, or our true being, should not be confined to a life within the body but once gone, free the spirit to continue on. To where? God has the answer, and we can only venture a hypothesis.

All the species are intelligent in one way or another, but only humans have been granted the capacity of consciousness of self, of their surroundings, their mortality. Only humans can project thoughts through the creative process, only they possess free will, the complicated language to express points of view, write poetry, literature, compose music, wonderful melodies, the capacity to analyze and philosophize, create all manner of instruments, and undertake scientific testing to discover the secrets of creation. All that and more thanks to those magical instructions, written in the chromosomes that form a marvelous cerebral cortex allowing us to carry out those surprising functions. If the Creator has provided us with all this, it would not have been only to entertain Him in observing the game of life. To watch us be born, grow up, learn, feed and educate our children, work, interrelate, enjoy and suffer, love and hate, fight against evil in order to get closer to goodness. And finally, for all the progress we have made during the course of a lifetime, all this information cannot just be lost when the body dies. The spirit retains that experience and continues on. This is my conviction.

If it were not so, then, all that perfection would be useless, without meaning, object, or transcendence. But it is unthinkable to conceive that all that has been built and may be qualified as miraculous, can be cut off in such a manner.

CHAPTER TWO

LIFE AFTER DEATH?

Does life of what we call the spirit continue after the body dies?

If we accept as real the number of cases in which a gravely ill person is floating in the ceiling, watching his body and all the details of the room, the answer is YES.

-A very profound and pleasant feeling of peace and calm and the perception of levitation in a narrow tunnel at whose end a very bright light is seen, the answer is YES.

-An encounter with deceased family and friends that welcome the person on the point of death, the answer is YES.

-An encounter with a luminous being, a quick review of the past, or the sensation of seeing oneself being returned to the body in spite of wanting to stay. Again, the answer should be a YES.

Skeptics believe that these experiences are produced by a chaotic chemical-electrical functioning of the nerve cells. Can chaos produce similar experiences in every case? NO. If so, it would produce disorganized experiences of all kinds and without an intelligible sequence; thus, the inevitable conclusion is that what is perceived is real, actually happening.

It is very certain that to the majority of humanity it is possible to perceive other levels of existence, but the restlessness and confusion of the mind does not allow it, these levels are so subtle that our five senses cannot capture them. Occasionally, putting aside the confusion of the mind and on looking inward in order to reach a state of complete relaxation, extrasensory experiences can be had, fleeting but real, of that subtle world.

Why am I so certain that life does not end with the death of the body?

Because I have had a number of experiences in which some of my loved ones, on the death of their bodies, and at my request, have given me proof that their spirit was there with me. Each one in a different manner, but totally convincing. Why has this happened to me? I don't know. Is it a gift? Just for me? I don't believe so. Therefore, I feel I must share my surprising experiences with whoever wants to listen to or read of them. The absolute certainty that life does not end with the death of the body has been revealed to me, and this certainty makes me see death not as a finality but as a new and interesting beginning.

There are those who can describe a person in spite of never having seen him, just by giving his name, age, and address, and I ask how can that be? And the answer is always: I do not know, it comes to me. A friend of mine, Venancio Vazquez, can do this, and he can prove it to anyone who does not believe it. It always surprises me, that special gift that he has, a gift from God, and I accept it as the irrefutable truth, in spite of the fact that I cannot do it.

We have proven on almost every occasion that he can describe a person, physically and mentally, even though that person lives in a faraway country. In less than a minute, he is able to make contact, and it takes him less than five minutes to describe that person, whom he does not know, living ten thousand kilometers away. How to explain this phenomenon? At what speed does the mind get access to this information almost immediately in spite of great distances? This only proves that the mind is not limited by distance or time. What laws apply in cases like this? Evidently, it would be fascinating to know.

Venancio Vazquez is not a fictitious character, and his clairvoyance gifts are real. He is a good friend of many years, and I have been able to observe how his capacity for extrasensory perception has grown, which he himself cannot explain.

A few years ago, maybe fifteen or more, he gave us, during his vacation, a free course in visualization and mental control. As a skeptic, I had no choice but to attend, for which I was grateful at the end of the course; I had vivid and marvelous experiences that convinced me that our mind has the capacity to reach other levels than our five senses won't allow us.

It was a five-day course, all afternoon and early evening, and as it progressed, our perception became more pronounced. On the fourth day, he indicated that we should now find our own spiritual mentors.

We were completely relaxed and receptive at the alpha level. I wanted to see my father as my mentor, but inexplicably, my mental screen was blurred with a beautiful violet-colored cloud, with vivid sparkling white lights which did not bother nor blind me. I was entranced watching that lovely cloud when suddenly, in the upper right hand corner of my vision; an intensely brilliant red appeared in the shape of Jesus' sacred heart.

I was confused because, in spite of being a believer, I was not much of a church-goer, and was aware that little figurines were sold representing the sacred heart, but I really had no idea of its meaning. Therefore, it was a vision that I could not have invented. Why should such proof of the existence of Christ appear to me when my few merits do not justify that marvelous message? What did it mean, or what had I done to deserve that vision? Perhaps the reason was to make me aware that Christ is love and He is among us. I do not know, but from that moment on I was absolutely certain of His existence and immortality. After much thought, I dare to divulge this experience, for it is important that I share it, to reaffirm in the hearts of men and women, believers or not, that Christ is among us.

I do not doubt that some will think that I lie, or that all is a figure of my imagination. But I am also certain that many will believe it, not because they think I am incapable of lying, but because they too have had similar experiences and do not dare to speak of them for fear of unbelievers mocking them. What would I gain by lying? Those that took the course with me, including Venancio, can vouch that I speak the truth.

The late Leonardo Pasquel Jimenez undoubtedly found peace easily. A good-natured, scholarly, upright and honorable man, convinced of reincarnation, and regularly practicing meditation, told me he had had the same experience. Why should a man who had left the Catholic church, displeased with its concepts - to him wrong – be convinced of reincarnation (in spite of the church's denial of it) and yet have a beautiful vision of Christ? For his benevolent behavior and surely because his concepts were not mistaken.

He commented that to take an astral trip, out-of-body, was perfectly possible. He never admitted that he was capable of doing it - although I think that he was - but he firmly stated that he knew some who had been able to. Why doubt his word? He also surprised me when he told me that he knew who he was in his previous life. Since I wanted to know more, I asked him who he was, but he responded: I can not tell you. I knew that such a man could not lie to me or any one else, since I could not doubt of his integrity, and knew that he had practiced serious meditation during more than twenty years. In spite of all, it is not easy to believe, but now, after many years elapsed I am convinced that maybe reincarnation is part of the plan of the Creator.

REFLECTIONS OF A BELIEVER

My father, very ill at the time, few days before dying, told me, upset, that he was fed up with frequently seeing himself hanging from the ceiling, viewing his body and the room he was in. He always thought that on the death of the body, it all ended there; there was nothing more. Fortunately, it is clear that he was wrong.

It is said that no one has returned from the dead. If they are referring to the physical body, they are right. Once dead, the body ceases to exist, is no longer useful, a shell of whose cycle of life has ended and should be recycled into nature. It has served as a vehicle for the spirit that abandons the body and passes to another plane of existence. It is the spirit that can manifest itself, that can give faith to its existence in a different more subtle manner. I have been fortunate enough to confirm this on different occasions and I am not the only one. As I have learned, those same experiences have happened to many others.

Why am I so certain that we have a spiritual protector? A guardian angel, so to speak. Because if it were not so, I would have died through the negligence of those in charge of warning drivers that a bridge had fallen on the Queretaro highway. I was driving calmly at a good speed, all seemed normal, when suddenly I heard a voice in my right ear shouting: BRAKE! Which fortunately I did not question, and did. To my surprise, I found a warning sign 10 meters from the hole. Burning tires, I was able to brake, and had time to take the detour on my left where I stopped, stunned. I did not think at the moment that I could have killed myself but rather that I was able to hear that voice warning me. Who warned me? Now I understand.

On publication of the first edition of my book, *Un Nuevo Amanecer* (A New Dawn), I was approached by a few persons who wanted to tell me of their own experiences on this very subject. They had not dared to recount them for fear of not being believed or being made fun of, but after reading the essay, they decided to tell me, knowing that they would be taken seriously. I won't go into detail on the subject, but I think a few of the stories are interesting.

REFLECTIONS OF A BELIEVER

A good friend of some years, travelling with his children in his car, suffered a terrible accident; he told me that upon reading my book, the part where Francisco had an accident, he suddenly started to cry uncontrollably.

Surprised, I asked him why, as I would have expected anything but that my story makes him cry.

He answered: Do you remember the accident I suffered years ago?

Yes, of course.

Well, what you described happened to me almost identically. After the collision, incomprehensibly, I was outside of my car observing all that was happening around me, desperate to know how my children were. I could see their inert bodies lying on the pavement; I wanted to know if they were still alive, something about them, but no matter how I tried, no one was aware of me. I was impressed that I could move from one side to the other on my own will without effort. On not getting any answer, my desperation turned to terror, for I did not understand what was happening to me. Then two figures that appeared to be hooded approached me; I could not see their faces. They told me to calm down, that my children were safe, and everything would be all right. I felt a great sense of peace at that moment, and that is all I remember. Fortunately, when I woke up in the hospital, after a long period of intensive care, I learned that indeed my children had suffered no injury after all. The similarity with Francisco's experience, as told in my book, *Un Nuevo Amanecer*, is amazing. That he could move from one place to another at his whim with no effort is very interesting. If that were so, it confirms that the spirit enjoys great unrestricted freedom to move to any place it desires on just the blink of an eye.

A person I am very fond of who suffered the terminal phase of a terrible cancer told me that the night before he had left his body and suddenly found himself in a beautiful garden with lovely sweet-smelling flowers, fountains of crystalline water, and could hear what he considered celestial music as well. What impressed him most was the wonderful sensation of peace, harmony, and well being enveloping him. He then made out some persons at a distance who told him that it was not yet time and that he had to go back. He thought that they were his father and dead siblings, tried to get closer to them, and was surprised that they made signs for him to not approach; it was not yet his time. Desperate, he begged to not go back, but it was useless as he then found himself back in his body again. After that experience, all he wanted was to return to that wonderful garden. Undoubtedly there are those who would think that it was a hallucination, for it is difficult to believe it was real. But, a hallucination that produces this range of feelings? I do not think so. He described the garden perfectly, with the surging crystalline water, the lovely flowers, the exquisite aromas, the supposedly celestial music, and the peace, love, and happiness that he had never before experienced. I would be delighted to imagine all this and experience at least the peace and complete happiness he had known. It must be marvelous.

On another occasion, he told me that the night before, he had an episode of terrible pain, unbearable, and suddenly found himself outside his body observing how he writhed in pain, but no longer felt it; it was his body that was in pain.

We made a deal. Whoever died first must give proof that his spirit did not die. When he passed away, I asked him to give me a sign that he was with me, but nothing happened. Two days later, about ten at night, his widow called me, all upset, asking for my opinion on what was happening. She had opened the closet where her husband's clothes were hanging, to select some for donation, but she was overcome with sadness and had to leave to sit down, as she could not control her sobbing, and, she prayed.

She was surprised when the key ring moved with force from one side to another, like a pendulum. She was stunned and noticed that the movement continued as the minutes passed, when she called me, fifteen minutes had gone by and the key ring continued swaying.

REFLECTIONS OF A BELIEVER

That movement, of course, was impossible without the intervention of an energy to make it move. I asked her to call her daughter and her granddaughter to prove that she was not hallucinating. She called them, and they saw that the movement was real. This phenomenon did not let up for forty-five minutes, so they were able to film it on video camera. The door to the bedroom and the windows were closed; there was no earthquake, so there is no material explanation for this phenomenon. Was that not the proof that he had agreed to? Without a doubt.

I was awakened one night with the bad news that a dearly beloved and marvelous person had died, one with whom I had great affinity, a spiritual identification. I was not surprised, for she was very ill. I hung the telephone up, but picked it up again wanting to let someone know, but at five thirty in the morning, it did not seem right to do so, so I hung up again. I then felt a presence, and asked that if she was there with me, to give me a sign. I was watching, thinking that I could see her. Nothing happened but what was my surprise to see the floor lamp that was beside my bed start to sputter with a beautiful blue light. The intensity increased and illuminated the ceiling to then lower and then increase again. That happened three times. My God, a short-circuit with blue light? That is not possible, and least of all when I checked to see that the lamp was not even connected. I was not frightened; on the contrary, I was filled with great joy. I thought that her spirit could appear, and if that were so, I would perhaps wonder if my mind might have been playing games, but it never occurred to me that it would manifest itself in that manner.

I was impressed to discover that in the Hindu religion, blue - very close to a violet color - is the equivalent of the awakening of the third eye which represents illumination. This confirms to me that this person possessed a very high spiritual level, which did not surprise me, for her conduct during her lifetime completely endorses it.

A good friend told me that he had been advised that a beloved brother of his had died, that all hope of saving him during the terminal phase of a long illness had been abandoned. Instinctively, without understanding why, he felt the need to ask for proof that his brother's spirit was nearby. Nothing happened at that moment, but suddenly, he saw the guard, the chamber maid, and the chauffeur, came running, livid and with contorted faces. What happened? He asked.

Sir, you are not going to believe this, but the entrance door was closed and we heard your name shouted three times. It sounded like the voice of your brother Juan. The dog went wild, barking and scratching at the door. They had looked everywhere but there was no one. This friend told me that his employees could not sleep well for a number of days. It was a shocking experience for him, but wonderful. He felt that if he had heard his name called, he might have doubted and thought that his mind had invented it. It was good that it had been others, who had not known of his brother's death, who had heard his call.

Another case: a friend, whose brother was on the verge of death owing to a ruptured aneurism. The doctors had practically given him up for dead; however, he miraculously recovered. Upon recovering consciousness, the first thing he did was mention to his brother that a friend from Monterrey, whom he had not seen in years, had died. Worried about his brother's mental state, for he thought he was delirious, he asked: how do you know?

Because I was descending and he was ascending.

What does that mean?

That I was coming down in to my body, and he was going up because he was leaving his. They tried immediately to locate the friend, and were informed that he had died three days earlier.

A very devout friend, believer in the Virgin of Saide, who as a young man lived in Lebanon, told me that he had once caught a pneumonia that almost killed him. He was so ill his parents decided to take him immediately to the hospital. On the way, he asked his parents that before going to the hospital, they take him to a church to visit the

Virgin. There he fervently asked that she perform the miracle of a cure, as his death would cause his parents much suffering. When he was admitted to the hospital his parents were informed that with the equipment on hand, there was little they could do to save him. He told me that in his delirium, he saw the Virgin approach his bed and lovingly lay her hand on his chest. Right away he vomited profusely. The doctors rushed in and were amazed to see that the vomit did not come from his stomach, but from his lungs and bronchial tubes that had expelled all the infected mucous that was killing him. He was cured almost immediately. The doctors could not believe it. They had witnessed a true miracle.

What happened after my best friend passed away was impressive. He was a virtuous, humane, generous, honest, brave, and very nice man. In the terminal phase of his illness, he informed me that he was going to reserve a penthouse for me on the other side. I thanked him for his offer, but made it clear that I was in no hurry.

As reasonable as he was, he did not like to argue, and it was impossible for him to do so concerning money, especially with family and friends.

He was in partnership with two brothers-in-law, one of which was in charge of managing the business. He had mentioned to me that the business was not losing money, but there was little profit. He never mentioned that he suspected this could have been because of administrative wrongdoing.

Now comes the inexplicable: A few days after he died, the son-in-law of a witch doctor from a nearby town visited the widow and told her: Madame, your husband came to visit me last night and asked me to tell you not to think of selling the business he had in partnership with his brothers-in-law, that it is an excellent business, but the problem is that the brother-in-law in charge of managing it has been skimming off the profits for some years now. What could one think? Was this man out of his mind? Was it true? Just in case, it was decided to carefully audit the business, and sure enough, it was found that the brother-in-law had been stealing from it over many years. Hard to believe? Undoubtedly, but it happened.

And why not share this? A few years ago, a tumor was detected in my epiglottis. I was operated on by Dr. Carlo Pane who I believe is one of the best ear, nose, and throat specialists in Mexico. He removed the tumor which fortunately was benign. My throat was under observation for some time, just to make sure. The third time I went for a check-up, he told me that I had leucoplast in the throat. What is that, I asked? It is a growth of an incurable white plaque, I was informed. How come it is not curable? There has to be a procedure for its elimination. His answer was straightforward: I told you that it is incurable, and can become cancerous, so throw the cigarettes in the garbage. To continue smoking would accelerate the possibility of cancer. It was hard to accept his advice, so I paid no attention and continued to smoke. Time passed and the inconvenient white growth was still there.

One day, I went with my wife to the doctor, as she was to undergo a minor operation. It is possible the tranquilizer they gave her was overly strong because she was still deeply asleep after the operation. I took advantage of this to go out to the street for a moment; I shamefully admit that I wanted to smoke a cigarette. While doing so, I was aware that a man of approximately seventy-five years of age was approaching me. He was tall, thin, with calmness in his eyes, and carried a shoeshine box. He came up to me and asked: a shoe-shine? Yes, of course, please, I answered. We started to talk and I asked him at what time he started and ended his working day.

I start at seven thirty in the morning and finish at seven thirty in the evening.

My! Walking twelve hours in a row should be tiring. Do you not get tired working so many hours?

Tired, boss? How can I get tired? I love my work, I have all I need, a roof over my head, and I am very happy.

What a surprise, I thought; I have met up with a wise person who shines shoes. A man who, in spite of his precarious economical situation, is truly rich and has what many never possess: happiness.

We continued chatting and finally he finished shining my shoes and without asking what he charged, I gave him a two hundred peso bill. He gave me a worried look and said, I have no change, boss. I told him that it was all for him, and that I was still indebted to him for he had given me a priceless lesson.

He looked at me then and said: God bless you.

Thank you, and may God bless you too. It was a magical moment difficult-to-describe, wonderful energy was felt. We parted cordially and I entered the clinic once again.

Two or three weeks went by and I returned to my customary appointment with Dr. Pane.

He checked me over carefully, and when finished, told me, stunned: you are in perfect health!

What do you mean by that?

That the white growth has gone.

I said to him: Hey there Carlo, you assured me that it was incurable. Why deceive me?

Carlo Pane, rather upset, assured me that he had not intended to deceive me, that in all his years as a doctor he had never seen a growth of this nature to be cured, and certainly not spontaneously. His reaction was to point upwards.

A word to the wise is sufficient. There is no need to go into detail on the subject. To believe or not believe is everyone's privilege.

REFLECTIONS OF A BELIEVER

Who has not felt a sudden hunch? I suppose that all of us have felt one at one time or another. A clear warning that makes us feel that we should not do anything as planned, in spite of having thought conscientiously about it, and which we believe cannot fail and is apparently perfect, and instead, it turns out to be a failure. Or on the contrary, we make a snap decision because our intuition tells us that it cannot go wrong, and it becomes a success.

I do not mean by this that it is not necessary to analyze what we wish to undertake. Of course, numbers are an exact science, but they do not solve problems related to the intentions of others, nor of the actions and reactions that arise in complex human relations, nor of the possible outcome of events.

Summing up, I believe that eventually we receive some sort of notice from our spiritual mentors. It is wise to listen to them. We can all be aware of them.

All is movement in the universe, nothing is at rest. A rock, for example, seems inert but that is not so, for it is composed of atoms that are in constant movement. All material, apparently at rest, vibrates. But, the more dense, the slower the vibration and by saying that, we arrive at the conclusion that different levels of vibration exist. In the vegetable kingdom it is more intense, in the animal kingdom it increases, even more so in human beings; not uniformly as it is proportionate to the intellectual development and the spiritual evolution of the individual.

On a spiritual plane, this vibration is much greater, the mass more diffuse and as such, we cannot perceive it with our five senses. Following this concept, I must think that on a spiritual plane, accepting the premise of as it is down it is up, vibration increases in accordance with the evolution and hierarchy of different spiritual levels. Upon arriving at the top it reaches maximum vibration - that of the spirit, the energy, and supreme intelligence of the Creator.

REFLECTIONS OF A BELIEVER

This is not a crazy hypothesis. If correct, it would explain why we cannot perceive the spirits - a diffuse mass and an intense vibration totally invisible to our visual capacity - that are surely among us.

Let us make a simple experiment: observe the motionless wheel of a bicycle; it is made up of a few metal spokes, perfectly visible; but if this wheel is made to spin at great speed, the spokes disappear from view. We know that these metallic spokes have not vanished; we cannot see them, but they continue to form part of the structure of the wheel.

There is a reasoning that has an apparent logic to it, in that it denies the existence of the spirit supported by the practical deduction as follows: a person who loses his sight becomes blind, and if his hearing is affected, he becomes deaf, or if his brain is damaged, he loses coherence, the capacity to interrelate with his fellow beings, or in extreme cases, remains in a vegetative state. Why may not the spirit intervene, if it is said to be immortal or cannot be damaged, and fill in for these deficiencies of the body? Thus, it is possible to conclude that without the body the spirit cannot function, for it is necessary to have a brain that allows it to perceive all the sensations of the organic senses. Once the body is dead, the spirit dies as well, for it no longer has the elements to enable it to perceive, and on not being able to see, hear, or think, it simply does not exist. This reasoning had me uneasy as well, for I found no answer to my doubts that would satisfy me.

By means of our five senses, it is not possible to analyze in a simplistic manner what is beyond our physical environment, or beyond the four dimensions in which we find ourselves imprisoned. Scientists have become aware that there are different laws of physics, one describing the macro cosmos and the other, called physics or quantum mechanics, tries to decipher the apparent chaos at a sub-atomic level, where the behavior of the particles do not obey the traditional laws of physics. As science progresses, solutions are found, but at the same time, new doubts arise. Now that more is known, we become aware of our increasing ignorance. As a naive person once said: I would give all that I know for half of what I ignore, which would be the same as exchanging his house for the whole planet.

Once our ignorance is acknowledged, we accept that we cannot rationalize something that escapes the capabilities of our intellect, and thus converts it into an act of faith. And why does it convert into an act of faith? Because we do not want to know about something we cannot see or touch, but that is there, within our reach, evident from the signs that are given to us in order to perccive that there is another or other levels of existence.

The experiences I have had over my lifetime have wholly convinced me that life after death is real. That the gift bestowed upon us to live a life in a body is to experience the great variety of sensations, mainly pleasurable, that life in a wonderful body offers us. To take on challenges, choose goals, take advantage of those gifts granted to us, to be useful in our surroundings, and provide our bit of help to enrich the lives of those close to us: in brief, to be able to feel compassion.

Undoubtedly, life can be difficult and can entail suffering, but suffering is a learning experience. If life were always a pleasure, nothing would be learned. The spirit, astral body, or whatever it is called, cannot correct blindness, but that does not mean that it is unable to see; it means that as a prisoner of the body, it has to suffer whatever the body suffers, enjoy what gives it pleasure, face the setbacks and challenges that life offers, and ultimately, tolerate and accept the limitations imposed by the body. The spirit should experience life in the flesh in all its aspects and possibilities and on the death of the body; it is liberated, preserves experience, and continues on the road of evolution, its identity intact.

In possessing free will, the human being is no longer an organism limited by programmed behavior. The human being has been granted the capacity to reason, the possibility of making his own decisions in order to overcome obstacles, or take advantage of opportunities that life offers, and be the only one responsible for his errors and correct choices. It also allows him to be led toward evil, envy, resentment, hate, greed or, on the contrary, generosity, love, understanding, and forgiveness. The former leads to suffering and the latter to happiness.

This liberty of choosing our way through life while in the body is what makes it so interesting. The variety of pleasurable or unpleasant sensations available to us are those that the spirit amasses and may evoke at any moment, even after the death of the body, for it is in the prison of the body where the spirit learns the experience of a caress; a glass of cold lemonade on a hot day or a warm fire in cold weather; the immense and delicious variety of flavors and odors that are enjoyed when offered; a baby's smile; the powerful pleasurable explosion produced by an orgasm; the solidarity and support of a good friendship; the deep love of a marriage; the marvels of nature. I could go on and on describing the wonderful gifts that the Creator has given humanity, but is it really necessary? Cannot life offer good doses of pain, tragedy, or failure as well? Of course, life is not all honey. One should know the bitter taste of life in order to appreciate its sweetness. A failure is a lesson which should build character, on the understanding that it is not only a lost battle, but an experience that can help you win it, if you know how to take advantage of the lesson.

Now then, something that I feel is really perfectly viable is how it is possible that a diffuse body can exist outside of an organism. It is evident that in that state, I suppose it feeds on Divine energy. Therefore, all it would need would be the capacity to see, hear, communicate and, of course, possess an intellect. Without the burden of a heavy body, it would be able to enjoy the absolute liberty of transferring immediately to any place it so desires.

How can that be possible? Only God knows, but it occurs to me that in analyzing the science of man, the cybernetic advances in which one computer can store an enormous amount of data, can produce a virtual reality, and in which are done an infinity of calculations at dizzying speeds using a now primitive technology; however, they now speak of atomic computing, that if developed would increase exponentially its capacity and make the current ones obsolete, as though they were being used in times of the caveman; or even more so, they are speaking of quantum computing as well, which would put the atomic computers to shame.

I wonder. If man can achieve this with his limited intelligence, how is it that the Creator is denied the possibility of doing this and more, when He has been able to create the marvelous organisms that exist in nature, a task, I believe, much more complicated than that of creating spiritual beings. How? I have no idea. Nevertheless, I am certain that the life of a Being persists after the death of the body, for the wonderful moments that I have experienced confirm this, and I would be foolish to not accept them as real, like an undeserved gift that makes me absolutely certain that the soul and the mind, on the death of the body, rise to other dimensions (not among the clouds as it is thought) among us and anywhere else they so desire.

I suppose there are laws unknown to us that allow this to happen, for it is evident that they are among us, although many of us are unaware of their existence, for they inhabit other planes that cannot be perceived by our five senses. Nevertheless, they are accessible if we go into our internal selves, modify the vibration of our conscience, and experience surprising proof of that subtle world. Therefore, it may be hypothesized that those diffuse spirits, in their bodies, can see, hear, communicate telepathically in an universal language, possess a sharp and quick intellect and store in their memory countless data, besides being able to go voluntarily to wherever they want, just by wishing to do so, as it may be assumed that they act on a spiritually mental level, on another plane or dimension, possibly quantum**, or spiritual,** free from the restrictions of space and time.

CHAPTER THREE

REINCARNATION?

I have always had doubts regarding reincarnation, but Venancio's vivid tale of his previous lives affected me profoundly. COULD IT BE TRUE? Why not! After all, it was mentioned in the ancient creed of the Church: I believe in the resurrection OF the flesh. Forgive me, but once the flesh is rotten does not come back to life. That is against all of the laws of nature.

How different it is to you say: I BELIEVE IN THE RESURRECTION IN THE FLESH. It sounds better and opens up the possibility of accepting reincarnation. A very alive spirit can go back to a new body created through the laws o nature: in the womb of a woman.

Ultimately, to believe or not does not convert us into heretics. It is possible that the first Christians did believe in it, and much later, it was denied by the Church, when in the sixth century, JUSTINIAN, master of the Roman empire and master of the church, IN AN ECUMENICAL COUNCIL, CONDEMNED IT. With what moral authority the church decides if reincarnation is valid or not? How can you prove one thing or the other? Could he have received a divine message that prompted him to make that decision? It is hard to believe, but if it were true, why would THE DIVINITY WAIT SIX CENTURIES

REFLECTIONS OF A BELIEVER

FOR ITS DENIAL? What WAS THE HIDDEN REASON THAT PROMPTED HIM TO CONDEMN IT? CONVENIENCE? CONVICTION? Who knows, but it is clear to me that it did not come from a Divine inspiration.

When a reporter asked the Dalai Lama: if I can prove to you that there is no reincarnation would you believe me? Of course, he answered, with a smile, but first you would have to prove it to me. I wonder how would a bishop react if you question one of his dogmas? Good thing that the inquisition is a thing of the past.

I was given a brochure by chance under the title of *Que pensar de la reencarnacion?* (What to Think of Reincarnation?) edited by *Buena Prensa A.C.*, publisher of the magazine *La Civita Catolica,* in which reference is made to the increase of believers of reincarnation in the Western hemisphere, taken from a survey made in European countries showing that twenty-three percent professed Catholics, twenty-one percent Protestants, and twelve percent "non-religious" believe in it. The article continued with a description of the origins of that belief and the reasons supporting it. Finally, by means of lame and unconvincing arguments, it was ruled out as absurd.

We all have a right to our own convictions, but on the subject of reincarnation, I feel that we lack the tools for arriving at the absolute truth concerning this hypothesis; consequently, since proof of one thing or the other is unattainable, reincarnation may or may not be ascertained.

The spirit is immortal? Yes? In that case, what does it matter if one is reincarnated or passes over to other planes of existence? That is in the hands of the Creator. Nevertheless, I think it important to reproduce the reasoning that lead to the affirmation of the absurdity of reincarnation that in my opinion, is quite questionable.

It says: if there is no basis for explaining all this by means of a hypothesis on reincarnation, whose absurd nature has been demonstrated, is there a possibility of finding some explanation to these questions?

REFLECTIONS OF A BELIEVER

In effect, we may find this answer to those problems in the Christian revelation. It affirms, above all, that all human beings have only one life, in which their eternal destiny is determined. But the fulfillment of this eternal destiny is not only man's doing. Salvation is really a gift of God that leads to fulfillment of the good that man, aided by Divine Grace, has accumulated during his life; and God forgives and revokes the sins committed by man. It is not, then, that man is saved by his own efforts, progressing from reincarnation to reincarnation, but it is God who saves him and makes him perfect. (Over and above what man can attain, through whatever effort he made over many lives, he would never reach absolute perfection.) It would be more appropriate to say: (achieve absolute love, since only God is perfect.) This is done by means of His pardon that, as the name implies, is an undeserved gift from Divine mercifulness. Thus men can save themselves, even at the time of their death, even though they have done little good and much evil; if they truly repent of the evil they have committed and trust in Divine mercifulness, God will forgive the evil (and in that way destroy it) and lead the good of the past to its fulfillment, by means of His pardon.

The Church does recognize that no one may be admitted to the sight of God if he is not completely purified. For that it admits to the doctrine of purgatory, a form of purification that enables the soul to envision God.

In conclusion, Christianity gives the answer to the problem of the destiny of man, overcoming the contradictions of reincarnation, that promises not only an evolving journey that never ends, but a face-to-face vision of God - immediately after purification in purgatory, if necessary - and AT THE END OF TIME, the RESURRECTION of the bodies that the spirits occupied in their life's. (This last concept makes me shiver.) Are we still in the middle ages?

I respect the optimism of whoever wrote that last part. It is a nice hypothesis, very reassuring, with the virtue of undoubtedly obtaining Divine forgiveness regardless of the behavior of that person during his lifetime. It offers a convenient solution, but would it be acceptable to think that an evil person could obtain the same reward as those who have tried to be kind and loving all their lives? I sincerely do not believe it. It would be unjust.

Only God has the answer. Why do they dare to affirm as truth a matter that is not within our ability to neither understand nor prove? Is it not illogical? It denies Christ's message, to affirm that the evildoers are saved only by repentance? Is it not said that Christ declared: by your deeds you will be known; by your deeds you will be judged; I am the road to salvation? I understand that to mean we should heed his message of love. Does this not annul the validity of WHATEVER THEY MAY DO, IF REPENTANT BEFORE DYING, THEY WILL BE FORGIVEN AND WILL ENJOY THE SAME PEACE GRANTED TO THE RIGHTEOUS?

Perhaps a sincere repentance would be an extenuating circumstance for qualifying the degree of evilness, but it does not liberate the evildoers from the damage caused and for this, there must be a process of expiation in order to expel the evil from their soul becomes necessary. It would be unthinkable that Adolf Hitler and his minions, or Stalin, or Beria would receive the same treatment as Mother Teresa of Calcutta.

And something more: all this does not tell us what happens to those that do not repent.

There must be many who did not have the opportunity of repenting, who died violently and suddenly, or while sleeping, or simply dropped dead without a word. To those unfortunates, will forgiveness be denied?

Since there is no answer to this question, we realize that this theory is incomplete, and absurd to me.

It is a consolation that no mention is made of the punishment meted out to the great sinners: banished to a horrendous hell, where it is said that the spirits would burn in an eternal fire. A concept invented by priests in order to control believers by fear of condemnation.

If it is said that the spirit is eternal and indestructible, how can it burn?

Is it not a contradiction to say that God is love, and then say that He can send His children to suffer horrors for all of eternity? Attempts to eliminate this medieval threat – which to my understanding is an affront to the goodness of God – are currently under way, for after all, we are in the midst of the twenty-first century.

We go to the opposite extreme when we say that we shall all obtain the forgiveness of the Creator if we repent of our sins, even at the time of death. This means that you may do as much evil as you wish since you will be forgiven if you repent. Is that fair?

As I see it, God gives us free will, but he has His laws, which are applied according to the conduct of each one of us. It cannot be so simplistic to think that we all will be forgiven in spite of the evil committed, and all, good or bad, will obtain the same reward. There is no hell, but evildoers, taking into consideration extenuating circumstances, should be purged through the suffering that allows the spirit to perceive the evil done, for in that state the evildoer is absolutely conscious of his wrong-doing, and that makes him suffer, repent, and little by little, forgive and free himself from that anguish. Nevertheless, his conduct produced a damaging effect on a fellow human being, and by law, in my opinion, the evildoer will eventually suffer the same effect that his conduct caused, and will know what it feels to be on the other side of the coin. This is part of a continuous learning process of evolution. If that is right, then there is no other alternative than to accept that reincarnation is needed for the evolution of souls. God does not punish. He who breaks His laws punishes himself, but that punishment should in no way be considered as eternal. There will always be another opportunity.

REFLECTIONS OF A BELIEVER

EVERY HUMAN BEING HAS ONLY ONE LIFE IN WHICH HE FULFILLS HIS ETERNAL DESTINY.

That statement seriously confuses me. How can a child fulfill his eternal destiny if he dies without not even having reached a year of age? Or two, or three, or five. Will this truncated life automatically be given the right to go to heaven? Would that be fair? He who dies at age one, two or five years, has no way of carrying out his eternal destiny, for he has not had the opportunity to show his goodness, for which it is necessary that he occupy a new body, live a long life, and show his tendencies toward love.

If we state that life in a body is a gift granted by the Creator, why should the spirit be denied the right to experience a reasonably long and fulfilling life if its body died at a very young age? Here again the concept of reincarnation applies, for if this were not so, the spirit would be cut off, both in the opportunity to transcend, as in the right to experience a life in the flesh.

If we state that God forgives everyone, including repentant wrongdoers, what do they call forging an eternal destiny if there are no consequences for their evil because they repented for having caused so much damage? Speaking of forging an eternal destiny, it is logical to understand that this would be the result of the conduct of their lifetime. On the contrary, how could we use the concept FORGING?

What may we think of the doctrines that have been taught throughout centuries?

Hell was invented to frighten and control the believers. Curiously, many of those that invented hell behaved in such a manner that they became the first candidates to go there; but they were not worried, as they knew it was a lie made up to intimidate the innocent. Later on, they doubted that hell existed, but for how many centuries and centuries was it upheld as the truth?

And then we have the famous limbo. He who dies without having been baptized goes to limbo. A measure to capture parishioners for baptism on pain of ending up in limbo. But they never explained what that blessed place was all about. Now it is said that limbo does not exist.

Why blame a defenseless baby because the parents did not baptize him? It would have been easier to threaten the parents with limbo. What confused mind pulled such an absurd concept out of his sleeve that only serves to make us doubt many others?

THE END OF TIME?

If time is eternal, it cannot have an ending. If there is a symbolic code in that assertion, it would be ideal if it were clarified, because on the contrary, that concept should be eliminated. It is clear that at that time it was unknown that the earth was formed approximately four thousand five hundred millions years ago, and that it still has at least two thousand millions years of useful life left to it before the sun initiates its final phase and consumes our planet. That would be the end of time on earth, but not of the universe.

If humanity has developed and evolved over approximately three million years, is it possible that the human race could exist one or two thousand million years more? Only God knows, although it appears to me highly improbable, for if in only seventy-five million years, evolution has advanced from the period of the great dinosaurs, to the first mammals, and from those, to the more sophisticated species, and finally to what we believe to be the sublimation of the Creator who programs human beings with all those marvelous manifestations of conscious intelligence. What genetic modifications can be expected of nature in only twenty million years?

What guarantee of permanence has humanity who is determined in destroying its environment and in producing more and more powerful arms of massive destruction, that in a moment of madness could erase humanity from the face of the earth? What new organisms would arise that would take the place of those existing?

The earth is also in danger of great cataclysms and among them, the most dangerous one will be the collision with some great asteroid that could wipe life off the face of the earth, although not completely. Would this be the end of time? I do not believe so, for after a while; life would flourish again, to continue on a new path of evolution, perhaps toward more perfect and intelligent, less voracious organisms.

Eventually the sun will consume the earth in flames and organic life will disappear. That will be the end of time of life on earth. Will that be the end of time as it is known to us? Two thousand millions of years would have to pass for the resurrection of the bodies, and curiously, if this were to come about, what use would it be because the hundreds of thousands of millions of those brought back to life would be burned immediately.

Now, it is said that Christ stated that there are many dwellings in the kingdom of His Father. That can be interpreted as planets capable of supporting life and I should suppose that those spirits can be transferred to another planet to continue developing in knowledge, love, and finally illumination.

New stars are being constantly formed, giving birth to countless planets capable of supporting life as we know it.

Why not think of the possibility that there are planets in existence where a happier life can be lived, with less evil and suffering? Where its inhabitants live in friendship and cordiality, and busy themselves more in the development of their intellect, and advance in the path of love, and that be its own reward for the more merciful; and for others where evil, ignorance and suffering abound, their punishment for having acted with malevolence will be a life with less favorable conditions for serenity.

All this is hypothetical, but how can we dare to speak of the end of time when we have no idea of what we are talking about?

The concept of the end of time was probably proposed by Paul of Tarsus who, following his inspiration, deduces that the end of time will happen in a thousand years. A thousand more years have since passed and fortunately Paul's inspiration was wrong.

RESURRECTION, at the end of time.

The brochure says:

There exists in man a desire for infinite happiness that cannot be satisfied by means of a chain of existences, but rather only through participation in an infinite happiness.

It seems reasonable to me to think that human beings desire infinite happiness, but how may they deserve it? God is a loving being that does not punish, but would He grant everyone the same reward, when so many have behaved in such a manner as not to deserve it?

It is also affirmed that the body be eternally happy with the soul, THE SAME BODY whose spirit lived in the flesh.

It refers to a body of flesh and bones. Of what benefit would it be to the soul if it is given the same body as the previous one? How can it claim to be eternally happy in a body that is mortal by necessity? It would have to be conceived in accordance with the laws of nature, in the womb of a woman. In that case, it would be REINCARNATED in another body, with the same characteristics as the one before: mortal, and subject to the same hardships and passions. It does not tell us of a body with different characteristics. What does common sense tell us?

Also, it does not explain to us at what age those bodies would resuscitate, and what is worse, about those that had the misfortune of occupying a body with deficiencies: mentally ill, handicapped, deaf, blind, paralyzed, mute, or deformed. Would a body with the same deficiencies be assigned to them? They affirm that they will get back to the same body occupied by them during their lifetime. For the love of God, what injustice!

Infinite happiness? A state of infinite and passive contemplation? This possibility does not seem too appealing to me, for it would be the equivalent of being uselessly alive.

When I was a boy, it was said that whoever went to heaven for good behavior would be in eternal adoration of God. Frankly, I did not understand why almighty God needed to have good souls in a motionless state, just in adoration of Him.

I believe that the spirit will always have a mission to accomplish in the Creator's work.

I find it interesting to quote Allan Kardec, whose name was Hipolito Leon, systematizer of spiritualism, and who brings up this concept in his book on the spirits.

What should be understood when it is said that the pure spirits are found united in the bosom of God, engaged in singing His praises?

That is an allegory that shows the knowledge they possess regarding the perfections of God, because they see Him and understand Him; but it should not be taken literally nor should many others. From a grain of sand, everything sings, which is to say, proclaiming the power, the wisdom, and the goodness of God; but do not believe that the blessed spirits are in eternal contemplation. That would be a stupid and monotonous state of well being, as well as selfish, in that their existence would be endlessly useless. They are free from the tribulations of corporal existence, which is a joy, and besides, as we have said before, they know all things and take advantage of the knowledge they have acquired in order to support the progress of the other spirits. That is their task, and a joy at that.

REFLECTIONS OF A BELIEVER

The body is called to resuscitate and join in the happiness of the soul.

Eliminating the possibility of reincarnation, and following the opinion of this brochure, we are to understand that eventually all those trillions of bodies would arise, with the same characteristics and needs of a human body, and as such, the question is: Where is the Creator going to accommodate all that humanity? With what is He going to provide food and drink? And if by some miracle the Creator were to provide that food, what kind of life will await them in those overcrowded conditions? How can they be happy in that environment? And what is sadder is that in either a short or medium lapse of time, all those bodies (resuscitated) would cease to exist, AND THEN WHAT?

We are told that the spirit is immortal. If it does not die, how can we accept that it is going to resuscitate? Therefore, it is logical to think that it is also inacceptable to speak of resurrection at the end of time, for how can an immortal resuscitate if it has never died? The body has been recycled into nature, and then, the real being, the immortal spirit does not die.

I repeat: it is said that resuscitated bodies will join the spirit, and live an eternal life? Supporting an idea that cannot be carried out, for if the Creator were able to perform a feat of that magnitude, it would be a punishment to humanity. There is no way to understand it as a reward. I cannot imagine living an eternal life in a body that deteriorates constantly. That would be a true hell: a few years of youth and then constant deterioration, until ending up totally disabled, useless, and plunged into despair. Truly hell. Who in their right mind would accept that possibility?

If it were thought that the spirit would be provided with a body with different characteristics, glorious and eternal - not of flesh and bone – would it not be a more logical and pleasing proposition? Let us hope so!

It is inacceptable to reason that the body and soul will come together at the end, for together they loved God, and this would be as though assuring that the body and the soul are independent thinking entities that can love or hate. The body, that marvelous organism, controls the vital functions and informs the mind through the senses. It does not hate or love, so it may be deducted that that function belongs exclusively to the mind or the soul. That concept is untenable and should therefore be ruled out.

I think it wise that those concepts be modified, which in my opinion are based on reasoning pertaining to the reign of magic, removed from logic, common sense, and an ignorance of nature's reality.

I think it interesting to quote a part of the conversation held by Peter Seewald with Cardinal Joseph Ratzinger, at that time Prefect of the Congregation of the Doctrine of the Faith, and now Pope Benedict XVI.

His Eminence, if to pick the fruit of good and evil was a violation which caused a radical change, the Creator very insistently warns in Genesis of another much bigger taboo, perhaps the taboo par excellence; concretely, picking the fruit from the tree of life.

In Genesis it is said that God placed celestial guardians – cherubs with swords of fire – to the east of Eden to guard access to that tree until the day of final judgment. The human being has been converted into one of us, says God in the text of the Holy Scripture, since he knows the difference between good and evil.

Now then, careful, lest you reach out with your hand and eat as well of the tree of life, and having eaten, live forever. Does this mark a last frontier? Does one's own destruction start afterwards with absolute certainty?

Cardinal Ratzinger replied that he wished to show Peter the traditional vision of this image as developed by the Fathers of the Faith. The teachers of the Church explain that human beings can only be denied access to the tree of life if, after having eaten from the tree of good and evil, their conduct places them in an unfavorable position. Something is torn from them that, if taken arbitrarily, can only turn into perdition. In response to this new situation, God says that human beings can no longer touch the tree of life because if they do, immortality would mean, in fact, CONDEMNATION.

In this sense, exclusion from the tree of life, linked to the destiny of death, is a blessing. To have to live eternally in the manner in which we now live somehow would be an undesirable state. In a life characterized by so much confusion, death continues to be a contradiction and is always a tragic happening, but also a blessing, because on the other hand, with this kind of life, eternity and the world would become completely uninhabitable.

A clarity of thought may be noted in Cardinal Ratzinger's answer who also, wisely, abstains from alluding to the concept of the cherubs with swords of fire to the east of the Garden of Eden, and especially to the famous final judgment. But he is clear in invalidating the concept of the resurrection of the body in order to unite eternally with the soul.

I feel obliged to insist upon the thought of eating fruit from the tree of good and evil. It is evident that the fruit of good and evil is not something that can be eaten. The conscience and the capacity to choose our mode of behavior is a gift of the Creator. He gave us free will. Therefore, if this is God's will, where then is sin?

We have been told that we are sinners that we are born in sin, the oft-mentioned original sin that we are innate sinners that we should always repent of our sins, and suffer on account of them. Should all this be interpreted as that suffering is good and happiness is something bad? It is not kind to frighten believers with thoughts that would inhibit the freedom of arriving at their own truth according to personal inspiration.

Fear traps the mind, and inhibits the intellect and the liberty of those who are caught in this attitude. There is no need for whoever lives in constant fear to go to hell, for his life is already a hell.

Suffering is not something that makes us rise above, but something that is, and can be understood as, a part of the diversity of life; it is a lesson that teaches us to appreciate the moments of wellbeing; it is not good nor bad, it helps us to mature, but not to reach salvation through fear and suffering; it is reached through love. Let us not be wrong and stay trapped in the truth of others, for that prevents us from searching for ours.

Toward the end of the nineteenth century, it was declared that all that was to be discovered had been accomplished. Fortunately, many disbelievers did not accept that position and thanks to them, surprising and unbounded technological, scientific, and academic advances were achieved in one century and which continue at a dizzying pace.

On returning to the subject of reincarnation, it is valid to think that if it were true, we should be able to retain the memory of our past lives. Why is that not so? Because it is supposed that each life should be unique, original, with different characteristics, diverse surroundings and challenges, and the mystery of what the future holds.

Let us imagine that we have the possibility of remembering all our past lives, with its good fortunes and its tragedies. I have the impression that this would cause great confusion in us, perhaps to the point of madness, and we would spend our time thinking over the guilt's and offenses of our previous lives, which would turn the present one into a hell. Above all, with the certainty that when we die we will be reincarnated, how easy it would be to commit suicide whenever we were unhappy with the present life.

The scriptures say that the apostles asked Jesus: Master, are you Elijah? Jesus answered: no, Elijah was among us and you did not recognize him.

Elijah could not have resuscitated for it is evident that his body had been recycled into nature. Then, who among those that were there could have been Elijah? Saint John the Baptist? On accepting that possibility, it is clear that he was reincarnated, for he was formed in the womb of a woman.

I quote Pope Benedict XVI in his book *Jesus de Nazareth,* pages 363 and 364:

On this subject we witness the conversation that three disciples have with Jesus while coming down from the mountain. Jesus speaks with them about his future resurrection from the dead, which presupposes his crucifixion. The disciples then ask Him about the return of Elijah, announced by the scribes. Jesus says about this: Elijah will come first and restore all things. Now, why is it written that the son of man has to suffer so much and be despised? I tell you that Elijah has returned and they have done with him whatsoever they want, as was written about him (Mk 9,

9-13). On one hand Jesus confirms in that way the hope of the coming of Elijah, but on the other hand corrects and completes the image of all that, identifying the awaited Elijah with John the Baptist, without even saying so; in the works of the Baptist the return of Elijah takes place.

If Elijah were John the Baptist, who was born from the womb of a woman, is it not clear that Jesus refers to a REINCARNATION of Elijah? And does that not prove to us that the spirit does not die? For if it was not so, the spirit of Elijah could not have been reincarnated in the body of the Baptist. IT IS MY UNDERSTANDING that this affirmation of Jesus confirms reincarnation as well as the immortality and uniqueness of the spirit.

Surely my interpretation of this passage is different from that of the Church, but interpreting the text as written it allows me to think that my conclusion is the right one.

CHAPTER FOUR

FROM THE UNIVERSE

A review of the universe starting at the origin of present time I think would be interesting. I speak of 'present time' because, to my understanding, the universe has always existed and is eternal. This present stage is only one cycle in the expansion of the universe, having resulted from a previous contraction, for it could not have come out of nothingness.

It is evident that our scientists, in spite of having made surprising advances in the knowledge of universal laws, find themselves still in the dark about many matters unknown to them. They do not even have the certainty of whether the universe is flat, curved, concave, or convex. Just recently they have discovered that a repelling force exists separating galactic groups at increasing speed; and therefore the scientists deduct that those groups will continue growing apart until the end of time, and if that be so, the moment will arrive, through the eons, when their fuel or hydrogen will be consumed. Eventually the formation of new stars would become impossible and consequently, of life in matter. A sad hypothesis, if accepted, would lead us to doubt about the immortality of the Creator, a Creator that can no longer create, for all practical purposes, is as if He did not exist.

Fortunately, it is just one of many possibilities, but as I understand it, the universe is cyclical, consequently it expands and contracts, and if each contraction and expansion takes one hundred thousand millions of years, what difference does it make, for time is eternal, and at a spiritual level, cannot be measured. How may I prove that the universe is cyclical? I cannot, but logic and my intuition tell me that this is how it should be. How may scientists prove that I am wrong? They have no certainty in their knowledge to prove it one way or the other. I least of all.

What should be recognized is the incredible curiosity of humanity that stubbornly wants to understand something that finally proves irrelevant to humanity itself, for one is speaking of tens or hundreds of thousands of millions of years, when, in a cosmic blink, the earth will have been carbonized by the sun, and life on it will cease to exist. Of course, through that curiosity, it is possible that new discoveries will be made, driving humanity to achieve great scientific progress in other fields that will eventually permit man to make interplanetary voyages, taking the seed of knowledge to other planets. I suppose that is the next mission of human intelligence.

Now then, if the laws of the universe were decided upon by God, and function throughout the universe, they are clearly perfect.

Without the repelling force in sidereal space, all would come together eventually, defeated by the force of gravity. But it does not seem possible to me that the Creator has forgotten that if the expansion of the universe were to continue indefinitely, it would then scatter into infinity, ending in a dark and freezing wasteland. I find that hard to believe.

Scientists, in spite of their advanced theories, have not been able to decipher just what the force of gravity is. Newton discovered its laws, but up to now, science has not been able to understand it. Now it seems that there also exists a repelling force that makes the intergalactic groups move away from each other. What a surprise! And to what purpose? Goodness! To avoid the collapse of the universe in a short cosmic time.

I wonder: how could that runaway expansion be slowed down? Only God knows, but it occurs to me that just as now expansion is necessary, I suppose that at some moment in the history of the universe, the Creator has designed a law that would reverse the forces of expansion converting them into forces of contraction. In that way the force of gravity would be magnified in order to stop the expansion, starting a contraction that I suppose would be accelerated, until all would converge at one or various points, creating a black hole of monstrous size, a mass that would exceed the possibility of retaining the black hole. The theory of cords of force **says**, hypothetically, that cords that vibrate, and have a limit of contraction and on exceeding that limit construct everything; they should burst into a great expansion. At that moment, all would be composed only of a plasma of particles and Genesis would begin again, following the same process and the same laws as before.

I understand it is very risky to state a hypothesis about something that is totally unknown, but it is clear to me that if we have faith in an immortal Creator, we cannot accept that all this wonder will come to an end.

A good friend gave me an interesting opinion, which is: all cause produces an effect. The cause: the will of the Divine Mind of the Creator, and the effect of that cause was the birth of the universe. Therefore, the Mind existed before the universe. That is a mystery that humanity will never be able to solve.

All that follows is governed by universal laws.

A habitable planet, such as the earth, is governed initially by the laws of chemistry, and when it is ready to support life, the Creator then takes care of what is really important, such as the genetic programming of life, always in harmony with the environment of the planet. The Creator does not modify the environment in one stroke. All must take the time that is necessary.

What would be the purpose of seeking to create all these wonders? In the vegetable kingdom: flowers with lovely scents, beautiful colors and designs; plants of every type and design, ornamental, edible and medicinal; a great variety of trees, some producing delicious fruit, others a different kind of nuts, some giving shade, others medicinal, or producers of spices, fine woods, others useful as firewood. In the animal kingdom: beautiful birds, some with song; predatory animals and those preyed upon; a display of beauteous, esthetical organisms, perfect in their surroundings. Truly a miraculous paradise.

Up to this point, animals already possessed a great instinctive intelligence, but they were genetically programmed to behave in a predetermined manner.

I suppose that He would have truly enjoyed viewing His marvelous work but should have thought that something very important was missing: He had to share all that beauty.

We all have a right to express a hypothesis, product of our inspiration, that cannot be proven but whose object is to clarify an idea that is reasonable to us. We are told that hell exists, and that it is inhabited. Who can prove this? Or that at the end of time bodies will rise to join the spirit. This affirmation seems to me to be outrageous. Why should I not be allowed to express my own fantasies? Fantasies that I feel are more acceptable than those imposed on us as absolute truth.

That humanity loves a fantasy has been shown in the resounding success of *Harry Potter, Superman,* or *Spiderman* and all those heroes; they are entertaining, without questioning their absurdity, for it is good to get away from reality for a while.

I should guess that the Creator decided that there was a need for an organism to exist that had the capacity of appreciating His work in all its magnitude that would understand and enjoy it. He then called the angels forth that had followed His instructions in the creation of the organisms already on the planet and told them of His decision: we have to program a new creature whose intelligence should be powerful enough to reign on earth over plants and animals; an immortal spirit will inhabit each body where it may enjoy the immense variety of sensations and experiences of a life in the flesh. On its death, the spirit will abandon the body, enriched with the capacity to recall at will all the accumulated experiences and sensations provided by that life. We will also endow this human organism with full consciousness of itself and its surroundings, the capacity of advanced language, of hearing, sight, taste, smell, and feeling in such a manner that it can experience all the sensations of the body as well as the capacity for analysis, imagination, a great curiosity, artistic and scientific sensibility; in brief, all those gifts necessary in order to construct a society, where different capabilities are distributed so that altogether they can form a progressive and balanced civilization; and to achieve this, they would also have the capacity to create.

Create an intelligent life, asked the angels?

They could procreate since we have taken care that their perfect organisms have the capacity to reproduce thanks to the genetic instructions we have programmed in their chromosomes. They could also, at some point in their evolution, modify the genetic instructions in an attempt to improve some of the species, or seek the elimination of a harmful mutant gene, but create life? No. That is only for us to do.

They could create intelligent machines that help in the evolution of humanity in all scientific fields, that would also serve to discover My laws, and as a result of that development, they could learn the messages that eventually, at the right moment, will be revealed to the minds that are mature enough to understand.

In order to appreciate this wonderful opportunity, it is essential to grant them the liberty to act as they wish: Free will.

The angels remained thoughtful and one of them was bold enough to say that this liberty would allow them to misbehave and self-destruct or destroy their environment, as had happened in a multitude of other planets.

Of course, that has happened as you have said, replied the Creator, but it is also true that in many other cases the contrary has occurred: civilizations that have sublimated themselves and have achieved progress and harmony, brotherhood, respect, and love amongst one another. Why deny some the privilege of experiencing a life in a body possessing freedom to choose, because others have failed? IT IS INACCEPTABLE TO MAKE THE PRESENT GENERATIONS RESPONSIBLE FOR THE FAULTS OF THEIR ANCESTORS.

The duality of the universe is basic in My creation. You all know that very well; a positive and negative energy exists; without that duality, My plan could not work. The basic trinity of My creation is: positive, negative, and neutral energy. If it were otherwise, the universe would not exist, nor would the atoms which are the bricks of all creation. Therefore, all My universe is dual: love and the absence of it, heat and cold or the absence of heat, light and the lack of light, goodness and evil, happiness and sadness, health and illness, strength and weakness, white and black with all the gray shades. We could go on and on with examples. Now then, in order to appreciate and know what light is, we have to experience darkness; in order to understand what happiness is, we should know sadness; in order to find out what is positive we have to experience the negative, and so on.

It would be useless to try and create an organism of such a powerful intelligence that would allow it to confirm, study, and discover My laws, to reason and analyze, to make decisions to face the eventualities of life, and after achieving that, to deny it the right of acting freely. It is evident that to justify our objective it is indispensible to give them the freedom of acting in accordance with their criteria. We should allow them to choose among the options offered by life, to act freely and decide the road to take, for otherwise, they would not have free will, nor could they experience the variety of life in the body and thus, the spiritual: How could they prove their choice of good and love, and renouncement of evil? How could they know that facet of My creation?

Lord, I understand that my question was a foolish one, said the angel.

No question is foolish, for the objective is to clear up a doubt, whoever has a doubt and does not have the courage to clarify it will never reach the truth.

You well know that the spirit that inhabits a body will be a prisoner of it during its lifetime, and it will not know that the true BEING is IT, not the body. Each spirit is unique, as important as the whole. Each body will be different from the others; none will be identical to any other. Diversity is what makes life interesting, and the objective is happiness, although that depends on each one, for if the blessings that I grant them are not appreciated then they will bring about their own unhappiness. Kindness and love will overcome evil and indifference.

And will he who allows himself to be defeated by evil be condemned?

Be condemned? How could I condemn them if they are My sons? I give them the gift of experiencing life in the flesh, allowing them the freedom of acting according to their will, hounded by temptations and passions that they should overcome. Would it be fair to condemn those that have been weak and have failed? How could life in the flesh be considered a gift when it comes linked to the threat of being condemned if it should fail? It would be an unacceptable cruelty. I love them in spite of their weaknesses, but they should understand that the objective, their task, is to overcome the base passions by means of a road toward love. True love that respects the freedom of the loved ones.

They would have to analyze their lives and each one would be his own judge for they will be granted the mental clarity to perceive their errors, and to be aware of the seriousness of their acts. This will make them suffer, repent, and eventually forgive themselves and be forgiven. But in their next lives, they will be exposed to suffer the same offenses and experience what it is like to be on the opposite side of the coin.

Even though they have some debts to pay, a life in the body continues being a marvelous and novel experience, each one different, where endless new situations come up that have to be resolved, attitudes that should be corrected, and if they have to experience pain or rejection, so be it. Everything is a learning experience channeled to the evolution of the spirit, and it is unimportant how many lives should be lived in order to arrive at the goal of absolute love. Love, as you well know, is the most sublime force of creation, the most powerful. Without it, the creation of higher organisms would have no sense nor possibility of existence, for evil would end up destroying everything.

CHAPTER FIVE

ON BIRTH CONTROL

Throughout my life I have had many doubts on this subject which I think are shared by many.

Abortion is murder, and bringing children into the world when they cannot be fed properly, condemning them to a life of practically guaranteed misery, ignorance, and suffering is an act of irresponsible cruelty.

How to avoid it? Sexual abstinence? How absurd. The Creator has taken pains to make the sexual act a sublime experience, especially when performed with love, and He gave us the possibility of enjoying it continually, not just on the days permitted by the rhythm method. But respecting the rhythm method is not, a form of birth control? In that case, it should also be prohibited.

During the past centuries and millennia, the concept of grow and multiply was needed because infant mortality was very high and average life expectancy short; illnesses, wars, and epidemics decimated humanity. To multiply was a question of life or death for the species. In the twenty-first century A.D. that concept is no longer valid. Why? The reason is evident. The uncontrolled increase of population would cause tremendous devastation on the environment. We are already at that stage. The pollution of the air, water, global warming, destruction of the forests and depletion of natural resources, among others, is ruining the ecological balance. A great number of animal species will disappear and therefore humanity (Homo sapiens) will have taken charge of creating its own hell, and digging its own grave.

How to avoid disaster? By using the drugs that science offers to avoid unwanted pregnancies. Birth control. Each couple has the right to decide how many children it wants, with the aim of giving them quality of life. 'Quality of life' for the children and in order to achieve that, 'quality of life' for the parents is important too. Indeed, these drugs are produced by nature, and therefore I think that the Creator anticipated that the moment would arrive when humanity would have a need for them. It is not a sin.

Why not avoid unwanted pregnancies by the use of contraceptive methods? That way, the crime and the danger of abortion would be avoided. Fortunately, many priests with a more open mind do not condemn the use of contraceptives, and many bishops have declared themselves against the policy of the ecclesiastic leaders, especially in Africa and Latin America, where the increase of population is alarming, resulting in a scarcity of resources which deprives everyone of the opportunity of a dignified life. Is it not proper to go against the clamor of the masses?

This leads us to a dead end. The Catholic church condemns the use of contraceptives, and at the same time, qualifies abortion as murder; and really it is, except for very special cases where the procedure is justified.

But the church condemns abortion without seeing that it too is guilty to some degree, for it appears that it ignores true human nature and temperament – as we are, not as it thinks or wants us to be.

On prohibiting that pregnancy be avoided – which is not a crime – believers obey because of faith in the precepts, and because of their own ignorance which makes them believe that by avoiding pregnancy, they are condemned. But humanity cannot control its nature and obviously unwanted pregnancies occur, especially among the young who, because of shame or other reasons, seek an abortion to avoid their parent's wrath. They then fall into the hands of butchers, and on many occasions, not only does the fetus die, but also the mother. A double crime that could have been avoided if it had been taken up in the Vatican Council II called by Pope John XXIII, with the objective of modernizing the church and bringing it up to date.

Regrettably, John XXIII died before concluding this objective and as a result, the decision fell into the hands of Paul VI who, after a thoughtful analysis, unfortunately put to one side the present reality of humanity, did not recognize human nature, rejected the opinion of the majority of the bishops, and decided against the use of contraceptives. How many hundreds of thousands of abortions could have been avoided if his decision had been different?

Would it not be more productive to seek a logical and humane solution to the problem brought on by this dead end, and avoid the threats that only cause harm by galvanizing the people?

If the Catholic Church insists in its condemnatory position, it should recognize that it is in great part the cause of women seeking abortion; therefore, it is the church's responsibility to find a solution to avoid considering abortion a crime. How may that be accomplished? By eliminating that damaging prohibition that especially harms those who have less, understand less, believe more in what the priests tell them, and fear more of damnation by not following the precept. Ultimately, it is only an imposition of human beings who believe erroneously that they are interpreting God's will.

On avoiding an unwanted pregnancy, a life is not destroyed, and a crime is not committed - that of the abortion of a living being. Common sense gives us the answer to that quandary.

Sex is not only a reproductive function; for couples, it also has a necessary unifying purpose. Why satanize it? Why ration it? With what right does the church legislate what a couple can or cannot do in affairs that are strictly private and of no one else's concern? That is the limit!

God gave us free will to act in accordance with our convictions. No one has the right to affect that liberty by creating laws of behavior that violate the natural rights of humanity.

Jesus Christ gave us many messages, but among them, I am unaware of any concept He may have referred to, at any time, about what is acceptable or not in the field of sexuality. He gave the apostles the task of conveying his message: his philosophy of love, faith in a loving God, healing and salvation of the soul resulting from goodness, helping one's neighbor, humbleness, certainty of life after death, and other concepts. But I find none where He gives instructions with regard to the sexual behavior of humanity. I have been unable to find some passage in which He suggests that chastity is a virtue, and even less one dealing with the subject of how many children a couple should have.

To what confused mind did it occur to require a vote of chastity from priests? An ordinance that I believe goes against the laws of the Creator, against human nature, inevitably leading to hypocrisy and cheating, and to hiding the faults of many priests, so that the appearance of false beatitude may be kept up.

I have no doubt that some priests fulfill this precept because they believe that on doing so, they please Christ, but it is evident that the great majority do not. By not recognizing this, and covering up those that sexually abuse youngsters is deceitful, a hypocrisy that seriously damages the church. It especially damages those many that felt the calling and act with faith and rectitude with regard to the teachings of Christ, and are horrified at the abuses that distort the contents of their sermons. Men, after all, who take shelter in the force of the power they hold over their congregations.

Why does Christ not come and put things in order in His church? Because it is clear that if God has given us free will, neither He nor Christ will interfere in modifying the deeds of humanity.

CHAPTER SIX

A BIT OF HISTORY

On one of my trips to Rome, I felt prompted to visit the tombs of the popes, which I had not done in spite of having visited the Vatican on different occasions. I was surprised to learn that in the tenth century twenty-five popes had occupied the throne of Saint Peter; it was a time when a pope died on an average of every four years. What happened? I found out by chance when I read a book written by a Jesuit priest that, among other things, covered that period of the history of the papacy, clearing up the reason of the high mortality of the popes during that time.

I found this information in the book entitled *MI IGLESIA DUERME* (My Church Sleeps) written by S. Freixedo, a Jesuit priest, who was expelled from the Order to which he had belonged for thirty years owing to his book in which he makes a critical study of the state of the church during the decade of the seventies in a respectful and constructive manner.

It is important for me to quote S. Freixedo.

The real sin.

Polygamy is more serious than the use of contraceptives and nevertheless, we see in the Old Testament that God permitted it among his chosen people which suggests that the mind of God is not so strict as that of the moralists. That God is much more understanding of human weaknesses, that God full of ire does not get upset in heaven because of man's liberal interpretation of the law in whatever situation, and He understands the will of the law-maker. God does get angry when a man acts against love, when someone abuses or harms another. That, basically, is the only sin.

Have the moralists given these sins against love the same importance that they have given to the sins of sex?

Is not our church rotten with sins against love? Personal sins, sins of institutions, those of superiors and of the hierarchy, sins of Christian nations against those less developed, sins against charity on the part of the Holy See. These are the great sins of today that are in detriment of the church and the world – the uncontrolled selfishness into which we have all fallen, that goes radically against the precept of love of all.

THE SINS OF SEX

If one controls sex, he will have no problem in entering the kingdom of heaven. How many good men have been isolated from a more intimate and profound relationship with God by this false law, believing that God is very angry with them because of weakness of the flesh. If we understand the Gospel, we see that Christ considers that there is much more danger in money than in sex, and because of that, His words regarding it are much harsher than those addressed to the sins against sex. That is because controlled sex is nothing but a deformity of love, while money can harden our hearts and make us selfish. Since selfishness is contrary to love, it is therefore the real sin.

We spend all our energy in not doing what the law forbids us from doing, in repressing this or that normal pleasure of human nature. When the time comes to do good, we are tired of avoiding the bad.

Bad behavior is only so because those that govern us have determined that it is. What is deplorable is that God is made responsible. With intolerable arrogance they say that it is the will of God. What special revelation enables many bishops, priests, and others to say that this or that is against the will of God?

It would have been much better to have listened to Christ when he said: Woe unto you, doctors of the law that impose burdens on man that he cannot support and you, but with the end of a finger, do not touch them. We would not want that the Holy See abdicate from being the guardians of the faith. But this guardian has to have a much more positive character and renounce all critical attitudes of today. The day Gregory IX, in 1231, instituted the fateful tribunal of the Inquisition was a day of mourning for the church. That anti-Christian doctrinal witch-hunt was organized then and ended twenty-one years later by Pope Innocent IV who admitted torture. Today, the good name of that UNIVERSAL FRATERNITY FOUNDED BY A DIVINE FORGIVER OF ADULTERERS AND PERJURERS is still tarnished.

MANIPULATED FAITH

Freixedo again.

A thinking person needs to have faith in the existence of a superior being. To think that God protects his creation, and is thus loving and fair, leads us to think of the possibility of eternal life for our being, in the spirit, once our earthly body has died. What happens when the body dies, where do we go? This is a subject that lends it to various hypotheses even though, apparently, none can be proven during our life on earth. Even theologians, in spite of profound studies, only touch on speculations on this matter (Theology, etymologically, is the science that studies God). And what they arrive at is simply the creation of laws of behavior that the laity should follow, whether mistaken or anachronic, for as they assure us, it is the word of God. The rules of behavior for achieving harmony amongst humans are found in Moses' tablets.

DOGMATISM DEFINED

Dogmatism consists of a tendency to always speak = *ex catedra* = and to elevate to the level of dogma things that are not so. Another tendency of dogmatism is the extreme ease with which punishments are meted out to those who are not in agreement with the 'dogma': one is declared heretic or is threatened with hell. Finally, the absence of dialogue in order to clear up discrepancies is also typical. Definitely, dogmatism is a manifestation of authoritarianism, the most dangerous of them all. When a half truth is elevated to the level of a truth and imposed forcibly on the conscience, or when a disciplinary order given an importance that it is far from possessing, then the conscience of the subjected, especially in those of a higher sensitivity, begin to feel a disturbing and profound anxiety that can become an inner hell.

THE FIGURE OF THE POPE

Once again I quote Freixedo. A bit of history

Has there been a pope throughout history who, when teaching as a universal pastor - although not wanting to speak *ex-catedra* - has been wrong, or at least has spoken with less exactitude? Yes there has been and moreover, quite a few. Leaving aside the famous question of whether or not Pope Liberius (352-366) committed heresy, a question of very little importance, we can, without much research, make a list of popes who have committed doctrinal errors, more or less serious, in the exercise of their mission. We will mention only those that explicitly taught or wrote of matters that, today at least, we cannot accept as truths even though they were born of good faith and a pious spirit, zealous of doctrinal purity: Saint Victor 1(189-199), Saint Zosimus (427-428), Honorius 1 (625-638), John XXII (955-964), Gregory VII (1073-1085), Gregory IX (1227-1241), Innocent IV (1243-1254), Boniface VIII (1249-1303), Nicholas V (1447-1455), Jules II (1503-1513), Paul IV (1555-1559), Gregory XVI (1831-1846), Pius IX (1846-1878), Pius X (1903-1914).

Undoubtedly, if a thorough study were made, a few more names of popes who have upheld doctrines that over time have proved wrong could be added to this list. Their errors would vary a lot: from the monotheism that Honorius (excommunicated and condemned because of his name by no less than three general councils) fell into; and from the excommunication launched by Saint Victor against the church in Asia for celebrating Easter festivities "incorrectly" (excommunication that was lifted immediately by his successor); up to the false teachings of John XXII about the obligatory wait for entrance into the kingdom of heaven until after the final judgment – a teaching that was proscribed in a solemn resolution by his successor Benedict XII; or in the syllabi of Pius IX and Pius X condemning certain aspects of modernism, that today are authentic manifestations of the modern spirit. It is enough to say that to understand that the popes, even though assisted by the Holy Spirit in an exceptional manner, are far from being infallible in the ordinary exercise of their ministry.

In order to help all those pious but ignorant souls realize their error - those that identify the Supreme Pontiff totally as God - we shall put forth here a few historical facts, which although already well-known, are nonetheless true, and will also serve to emphasize our argument.

Confining ourselves to the end of the IXth century and to all of the Xth, the black century of the papacy, we may present the following pontifical picture:

While in the XIXth century there were only six popes and eight in the XVIIIth, in the Xth century, because of the prevailing chaos and the frequent forced removals from office, the number of legitimate popes reached twenty-five. In less than a century at least seven popes were assassinated and not exactly as martyrs but because of abuses they had committed or because of their rivals' political ambitions. Four of the supreme pontiffs ordered that their immediate predecessors be murdered in order to seize the pontifical throne. One, Formoso the Portuguese, in spite of his very honorable reputation, was despised so much by his successor, Stephen VI, that he was disinterred nine months after death, judged lying in state and declared an anti-pope, and his putrefying body was dragged through the streets of Rome and thrown into the Tiber River.

One pope, John XI, an illegitimate son of Pope Sergius and the diabolic Marozia, ascended to the papal throne because his mother had Pope John X imprisoned at Saint Angelo castle where she had him put to death by asphyxiation. A grandson of that woman assumed the pontifical throne; he was John XII, a man of many vices, elected when he was eighteen years old. Benedict IX was elected when he was twelve years old. Boniface VII stole all the gold and silver he could from the Vatican treasures and fled to Greece where he led a licentious life for some years. When he ran out of money, he returned to Rome, dethroned and jailed the reigning pope, left him to die of hunger in Saint Angelo, and proclaimed himself the new pope. His excesses were such that the masses rebelled, strangled him, and dragged his nude body through the streets of Rome. Gregory VI was – self-admittedly – a simoniacal pope. Benedict VI was beheaded in jail by the brother of the preceding pope. Thirteen popes did not last one year each in the Holy See. There were years in which three different popes occupied the Chair of Saint Peter in one year. And all that in one century!

It is true that all these events fill our civilized minds with horror, minds so distant from the barbarous methods of those times; nevertheless, we see this same mundane spirit - an excess of luxury and ostentation, far from austere customs, and an open politicking around the throne - reappear in many popes from the XIth, XVIth, and XVIIth centuries although of a character more harmonious with its time, but no less fateful for the church (and an example of that was the Protestant Reformation). But it is fair to admit that included amongst these popes, THERE WERE ALSO GREAT AND SAINTLY MEN who wore the tiara with utmost dignity.

Far be it from me to want to discredit the papacy, but also far from me is a pure mind keeping me from seeing reality and losing the historic perspective of institutions and peoples of this world. I have wanted to make this long digression in order for us to understand that all those popes, whom we see acting throughout history were no lesser popes than our present ones, nor did they have less aid from the Holy Spirit; nor did many of them rule with less thought and consultation before avoiding erroneous and inopportune results later. We are very sure that Paul IV, an honorable and extremely austere man, did not start a war against Philip II of Spain in defense of the Papal States, but did so only after a mature examination of the reasons that supported it. On believing Paul IV that Spain was a possession of the Papal States, something of a divine right (first mistake), it was logical to defend them by means of arms (second mistake), and it was easy to rapidly expel the King of Spain from them (third mistake). The crushing defeat that the catholic King of Spain inflicted on him (of course well counseled by Melchor Cano, the two Sotos, and the best theologians of that time) probably would have made the Pope suspect that the inspiration of the Holy Spirit was not a very good one in this particular case; and not only that, but probably he had his first doubts about the providence of God on seeing that He was so unconcerned about his States that He allowed an intruder to seize them.

Today, totally free of passion, and judging history with purely critical eyes, we can see that Paul IV was wrong in thinking that the pontifical possession of the Papal States were so by divine right (a mistake that Pius IX specifically also made), and that he did not act very much according to the Gospel by sending men to their death in order to defend a piece of land, and finally we see that the inspiration he had for expecting to win the war leaves the Holy Spirit in a very poor position as a strategist. If we carry to an extreme the inspiration of the Holy Spirit in all and every one of the acts and teachings of the Supreme Pontiffs, and if in each one of their dispositions we notice special assistance from Christ, we are accepting something very dangerous: we would have only to admit that neither the Holy Spirit nor Christ has played a very important part throughout history as advisors. It is therefore unacceptable to admit that the Holy Spirit or Christ is interested in taking the popes under their guardianship by the simple fact that they occupy the throne, which prevents them from using their free will. All the history of the papacy and even the church proves it. We shall not deny special aid but we affirm that the margin of error is still very wide for God rules the world, including His church, mainly by means of the intelligence of man.

A typical case of the confusion created in the minds of Catholics is the mixture of what is strictly revealed with what is deduced from that revelation by the processes of human thought and on indiscrimination mixing what is serious with light thinking. We may note in the Encyclical Letter number nineteen, of the *Humanae Vitae*, where the Pope calls previous prohibitions and dispositions regarding marriage divine law. In reality, what he defines as divine law is no more than a philosophical deduction of natural law. Undoubtedly in this world the term 'divine' can be applied to everything. But it is unquestionable that the divinity of those directives regarding marriage is very different from the divinity of all the order of grace and redemption. We quite simply do not admit that they be divine but very human, and consequently subject to human discussion.

Because of problems such as those created by *Humanae Vitae* in all of the church, one asks up to what point do the attributions reach that Christ gave the hierarchy. Because of dispositions like this, one sort of awakens from a dream and realizes that the hierarchy - taking advantage of its divine mandate and the sacred fear that this inspires on people - has acquired over the centuries, with the best of intentions, a stronghold on the intelligence and, even more, on the spirit of men.

The impression is given that the moralists, over the centuries, have been more papists than the pope, have been more moral than God, have made the law more restrictive, just as those hypocrites did, who were so criticized by Jesus. They have imposed terrible burdens on the shoulders of this fragile and weak humanity who carries all alone the weight of iniquitous laws invented by who knows what Freudian motivations in the sub-conscious of many moralists.

Up to here Freixedo.

REFLECTIONS OF A BELIEVER

We should not make the mistake of blaming those condemnable acts that have been committed throughout the centuries on all the members of the church. Wars in the name of God? The Holy Inquisition? Assassinations with the object of usurping power? The betrayal of the Templar's instigated by Philip IV, who was deeply in debt (a large amount was owed to the Templar's) because of his wars against England. How to overcome that economic difficulty? The solution was to accuse the Templar's of heresy and judge them by means of the Holy (?) Inquisition. Obviously by using torture; who could withstand such terrible torment? Stop, and I will confess whatever you want. Once heresy was accepted, the debts were cancelled and the Templars' properties confiscated. The pope made it known that the Templars only answered to him, but Philip (the Handsome) paid no attention to the papal displeasure, for which Pope Clement V, fearful that Philip would take over all of the Templars' goods, joined in the betrayal in order to not be left without any bounty. He started trials against the Templars knowing that it was an injustice to treat an Order in this manner that had spilled so much of its blood in defense of Christianity.

On March 18, 1314, Jacques de Molay, Master of the Order, heard the sentence that condemned him to life imprisonment. At that moment, he retracted his previous confessions made under torture and proclaimed that the heresy he was accused of was false and that the Order of the Templars was saintly, just, and Catholic. All those in a situation similar to his agreed to this new confession. They were then declared as relapsed for which there was only one punishment, to die by burning at the stake. That same night he was put to death together with another 35 Templar knights on the Isle of the Jews in front of Notre Dame in Paris.

In other Templar provinces, the reactions were varied but never was there any case of violence such as in France.

Or the cruelty of Innocent III, who wanted that all form of Christianity, should recognize the Roman pope as the supreme pontiff. Unable to convince the Cathars from the south of France, who repudiated the pope for not conducting himself in a Christian manner, he had thousands of them beheaded by his armies, until they were forced to accept his will.

Or the Borgia's. A period of a libidinous, incestuous, and criminal papacy.

Freixedo continues:

Speculations about this subject. Theology, etymologically, is the science that studies God, and what they arrive at is simply the creation of laws of behavior that the laity should follow, whether they be mistaken or anachronic, for according to them, it is the word of God. The rules of conduct appear in Moses' tablets for achieving harmony amongst humans.

Freixedo bravely dares to outline in black and white a situation that has prevailed over time, and clamors for a change that would place the church in modern times, with concepts in harmony with a new mentality. On pain of losing parishioners (as has been occurring) who can no longer accept the idea of a judgmental attitude that in reality is not what Christ would have them do, these changes must be made, since their true reason of being is that of nourishing faith in God and in the message of love that Christ brought us. A labor that belongs to the world of the mystical, not the mundane. A labor of COMPASSION, not passion.

CHAPTER SEVEN

A REFRESHING BREEZE IN THE DESERT

Pope John XXIII, the good pope, tried to modernize the church in the Second Vatican Council. He was the first to decide on breaking with tradition and leave the Vatican to get close to the masses, ending centuries of pomp and papal inaccessibility. He accomplished very little because he died sooner than expected, and the process fell in the hands of the papacy of Paul VI who also continued visiting different nations, but in my opinion, committed the mistake of clinging to ecclesiastic tradition. On dealing with the subject of contraceptives, in spite of the fact that many bishops appealed for permitting the use of these because the population explosion in Africa and Latin America was becoming a serious problem, he decided against it, attributing his decision to divine inspiration.

Paul VI died, John Paul I took over, and passed away mysteriously not two months into his papacy.

Then comes the papacy of John Paul II. He makes a definite break with the tradition of inaccessibility to the Pope and makes it his mission to reach out to the common people. Multitudes hail him. What an invigorating change!

He meets with the leaders of different religions, legitimizing the freedom of worship.

His pilgrimage was a constant one. Everywhere he went he was received with admiration, love, and joy. A charismatic man, great politician, and accomplished actor. In spite of the flattery, I would suppose that he remained centered. He worked until the last breath of his life, supporting and overcoming constant suffering because his failing organism made him so ill. A man of iron will, of absolute dedication to his mission. The people loved him, but unfortunately, this love was only directed to John Paul, not to the dogmas of the Church. Why?

It is important to recognize and applaud the labor of all those true Christians – thousands, or hundreds of thousands, or perhaps millions – who have dedicated their lives with love, with devotion, and absolute vocation in helping their fellow man. Among them are the missionaries with the Christian calling to aid the needy while facing dangers and lacking in material things. They shine like the sun in the darkness of evil and indifference. They give effectiveness to the message of Christ.

I just have to mention Mother Teresa of Calcutta. What better example of Christian dedication in helping the ill and the needy? She dedicated a great part of her life caring for the lepers of Calcutta with the help of many others whose compassion helped them to overcome the horror of that disease while ignoring the possibility of infection. What power of calling together, what magnetism must she have possessed in order to also found those shelters for AIDS victims, and gained the cooperation of persons willing to attend to them? A true saint. A demonstration of what real Christianity means, capable also of bringing forth the true kindness in humanity. What an enormous privilege to have known of her work during my lifetime but how many other Mother Teresa's are there, proportionately, who exist and have existed and of whose saintly work we are unaware of? It is true that she alone could not have achieved her objective, but fortunately, people who felt the same devotion, the same compassion toward the sick, surrounded her. What would she have accomplished without this help? May God bless all those that helped in order that this marvelous work be carried out, showing us that kindness and love prevail in this world.

There have also been many men who have reached sainthood because of their deeds, and many of them are recognized as capable of making miracles happen. Among them is the Lebanese monk, Saint Charbel, a true Christian, a saint of many miracles, or Monsignor Guizar y Valencia in Mexico. Inexplicably, the bodies of both did not decompose for many years.

It would be quite a task to investigate and make mention of the many who deserve recognition for their kindness, but to do so would fill many volumes because those who have distinguished themselves by their dedication is so extensive.

During my life, I have met many persons, generally good, others difficult, envious, greedy, some unreasoning, abusive, confused or arrogant but fortunately, I have not yet met up with someone who could be qualified as evil.

And why not? A person, a general practitioner, now deceased, whom I had the honor of calling my friend, had a true clinical eye, an ability for accurate diagnosis, and who could have distinguished himself among the best if he had wanted to; but he put aside the accumulation of riches in exchange for making a mission of his profession, which gave him great satisfaction – that of serving the needy.

When I eventually visited him because of a health problem, I found his waiting room full of people of little means. He took care of everyone, and if someone could not pay the laughable sum that he charged for his services, it did not matter; not only that, if they did not have money to pay for the medicine, he gave it to them. If someone asked him to make a house call, because the patient was too sick to go to his office, he always went however distant it was, or even if he was paid or not.

What a privilege to have known him. My admiration, respect, and affection go out to this true Christian: Doctor Miguel Jose Aiza, an example of love and compassion toward his fellow man.

No doubt there is evil in this humanity of ours, but love is more abundant, it is the force that allows mankind to prevail in time.

CHAPTER EIGHT

STUDY GOD?

How can God be studied? I could not, myself nor anyone else, explain it.

I have no doubt whatsoever that a Supreme Being exists, a great spirit, an intelligence of a size none of us could comprehend, that is manifested universally. On saying this, we are to understand the whole universe. Do we have by chance some certainty of what the universe is, what its dimensions are?

Do we know all of its laws? No. If it is said that in our galaxy, called the Milky Way, there can exist from one hundred thousand to four hundred thousand millions of stars, it is important to understand the meaning of this statement. It is estimated that our galaxy has a diameter of approximately one hundred thousand light years. That means that in order to cover it from one side to the other, we would have to travel one hundred thousand years at the speed of light. Now then, astronomers have no idea of how many galaxies exist in the universe, but they suppose that there are more than two hundred thousand million of them, and of course this number could be much higher. Therefore, if we multiply one hundred thousand light years by two hundred thousand millions of galaxies, we get a total of two, followed by sixteen zeros, and this without counting the intergalactic space, nor the sidereal space among the galactic groups. Unimaginable distances, are they not? To give us an idea, the light of the sun takes eight minutes to reach the earth, and in those eight minutes, it passes through the orbit of two planets: Mercury and Venus.

If there were a planet earth for each million stars in the galaxy, we would be speaking of approximately two hundred to four hundred thousand with intelligent inhabitants of different levels of intellectual development, some more and others less than ourselves. Now then, if we would venture to multiply these two hundred or four hundred thousand earths by two hundred thousand or four hundred thousand millions of galaxies, whew, what an exorbitant amount we would obtain! If there were only a planet earth in each galaxy, we would be speaking of two hundred to four hundred thousand millions of planet earths.

But. And if our universe were not the only one?

On affirming that the Divinity is present in the whole universe, we realize the insignificance of our marvelous planet at a universal level, that small planet where life swarms with innumerable perfect organisms in a wondrous ecological balance.

It is my conviction that the planet earth is not the only one possessing the possibility of supporting life and therefore it is clear that this miracle could be repeated in all and every one of the habitable planets of the universe. Why cannot life exist on planets with different characteristics that generate their energy by metabolizing other elements?

Bacteria have been found right here on this planet that have been baptized with the name of *Archaea*, the ancient ones, which scientists have determined go back to more than three thousand million years, when the earth was hot and covered with volcanoes and poisonous clouds. They were first found in the thermal waters of Yellowstone Park where the liquids are as corrosive as the acid of batteries; then found again at the bottom of the deepest oceans living close to underwater volcanoes in complete darkness, happily swimming in boiling water under an atmospheric pressure 245 times of that on earth. They love carbon dioxide, are poisoned by oxygen, can live in freezing regions and from there pass on to the highest of temperatures in volcanic lakes with a PH equivalent to that of sulphuric acid. And on top of all that, bacteria that swim easily in a nuclear reactor with radioactivity that would kill a man immediately.

How many more surprises will humanity come across as scientific investigation continues? I have no doubt that these bacteria were responsible for the cleansing of the waters and the air, ingesting and transforming what was toxic into innocuous elements allowing the plants to proliferate, and later on, these plants produced oxygen that oxidized the iron and fed the water and the air with oxygen that allowed the creation of aerobic organisms, a process that must have taken more that a couple of thousand of million years.

I wonder, does the Divinity care for only planet earth? I do not think so, for His laws are manifest in all of creation. Then we ask: how can we study the divinity that is manifest in the entire universe? It would be like asking an ant to study and understand the law of relativity; it is then clear I believe - although I hope to be wrong - that the idea of studying God exceeds human possibility, for perhaps on another level, on another spiritual plane, the glory of the Creator may be perceived.

Now then, if we interpret theology as faith in search of comprehension - in different fields, and with different possibilities - then it can be deducted that we are all theologians for we seek the comprehension of His creation. He has given us intelligence capable of understanding that, and thanks to the different gifts that humanity possesses; it may study his Creation and continue discovering His laws.

In that case, we are trying to understand His creation, which is an obligation of humanity; that is the reason He bestowed intelligence upon humankind.

CHAPTER NINE

CAN WE UNDERSTAND GOD'S JUSTICE?

It is odd how people think that God is somehow to blame for the tragedies of humanity. When an enormous quake occurs in the middle of the ocean originating a *tsunami* and, as a result, hundreds of thousands of people die, it is easy to blame God for not having prevented that catastrophe. Earth is a living planet, constantly changing, and this disaster was caused by a cataclysmic volcanic eruption, or by the movement of the earth's plates. Eventually the plates unlock, and the energy generated by this separation is such, that water bursts ahead through the ocean to the misfortune of the beaches that this swell unloads on.

Hurricanes and volcanic eruptions cause damage, but also work in favor of the continuation of life - they are much more beneficial than harmful.

A person dies and they say it is the will of God. Yes, in a certain way it is, because the death of the body is a certainty, but that person did not die at that moment because God determined he should.

An inebriated teenager drives at high speed, crashes, and dies. It cannot be said that it was the will of God. It was that young person's carelessness that killed him and luckily he did not take anyone with him.

If a plague destroys humanity, it is not because God sent a punishment. Humanity's ignorance and lack of hygiene were the cause of cholera, as was the plague that devastated and decimated whole populations during the Middle Ages. AIDS is the result of sexual perversion in this same humanity. Why did the Creator allow such a dangerous and mutant virus to develop? Would it be his purpose to punish homosexuality? I don't believe it. It is absurd to think that the Creator occupies Himself in modifying a virus with the intention of punishing someone. This is a result of the workings of the laws of nature which through mutations that eventually create a virus capable of originating a pandemic.

Could homosexuality not be the product of an organic, hormonal, and psychological imbalance that induces a man or a woman to prefer those of their own sex? Or that two men, or two women, fall deeply in love and decide to live together as a couple: if this situation is a product of their own creation, why should they be punished if they are not to blame for being different?

How can God be blamed for all those sailors that died of scurvy because they did not know that fruit containing vitamin C was lacking in their diet?

It is clear that there are pathogenic elements that threaten our health; this is only one, among the many other characteristics of nature, but we should recognize that we have been endowed with a miraculous immune system that allows us to resist illness. Some get better and others die. Is that unfair? I believe it has nothing to do with justice. It has to do with the law of survival of the fittest, which ensures excellence of the species.

In order to state an opinion about the justice of the Creator, it is important to know His laws. This is a subject beyond me, and I could not venture an opinion, but I suppose that all apparent injustices have a reason for being, are contemplated in the laws of the Creator - of which I am unaware - but it is unquestionable that a loving Being cannot be unfair, and everything must have a reason for being.

He has granted us all the elements to live a life rich in possibilities, in a world where the glory of the Creator is manifested in nature full of beauty and harmony, itself a gift to the marvelous senses with which He has blessed us. Is this not an irrefutable demonstration of His love for us? Is it possible to think that He, who has taken great pains in providing us with the means to find happiness, could be unfair? Of course not. Then, how may we explain these apparent injustices? The differences that exist between one and another: some healthy and others not, some enjoy themselves while others suffer, some are rich and others poor, as well as the differences in levels of intelligence. There are those that suffer a number of tragedies within the family, while others do not. Anyway, this famous duality does not justify these notable differences; therefore, there must exist laws that we are unaware of that can explain these inconsistencies. But, how?

As a key point, we should understand that the death of the body is a reality, but the true Being DOESN'T DIE. Undoubtedly those that loved the deceased suffer from his absence. For the deceased there is no tragedy, for the death of the body allows one to transcend to another plane of existence, in spirit, for that is the true Being, the immortal I, that inhabited that now inert body, and continues on to new experiences.

I insist, if this were not so, then all this wonder would be a useless, cruel, unfair, and absurd creation, without sense or utility. But fortunately this possibility is categorically ruled out because all that manifestation of sublime intelligence cannot be a product of a stupid coincidence. Consequently, a creative guiding intelligence is evident that undoubtedly must have a planned objective in order to elevate His creation beyond our understanding.

But, we ask: if God is love, why do we have to suffer?

Generally, we suffer because we want to. God has given us a paradise, and many of us try to convert it into a purgatory. We let ourselves be led by passions that poison our happiness. We envy our neighbor for all of the reasons that we can think of, we are obsessed by what we do not need, we do not count our blessings, we fall into resentment and wrong judgments, criticize our fellow human beings without reason, and we arrive at erroneous conclusions that cause us anxiety. "Live and let live". The stronger takes advantage of the weaker, of the ignorant, when it should be the reverse. Lying is endemic, especially in those that hold power, whether it is civil, economical, or ecclesiastical; undoubtedly power favors corruption. We could continue almost *ad infinitum*. All are a product of the justice or injustice of mankind, not of Divine justice.

A few years ago, I was on my way to my office, very upset because I had not been able to solve some matters which had contributed to my bad mood. On turning a corner of a street near my office, I came across a man, of about forty years old, moving around in a wheelchair with a tray full of candy for sale. Both his legs had been amputated. I was moved, but on looking at his face, I was surprised by the cheerfulness and happiness that radiated from it. How was it possible that he, without legs, could convey such happiness? Anyone would have wrongly described him as handicapped. Is not a handicapped person someone who has a healthy, complete body but is incapable of feeling that happiness, that ability to enjoy life so evident in that man without legs?

I was ashamed of my bad humor. I approached him to buy some sweets, and told him to keep the change. He stared at me reproachfully and said: sir, I sell candy, not expecting a hand out. I apologized for my lack of tact, blessed, and thanked him. From that moment on, whenever I feel upset, the memory of that wonderful person comes to mind, and like a balm, the tension disappears.

Now then, one may ask: why do some suffer hunger while others spend fortunes to lose weight? This is also an example of human selfishness, for nature produces food in abundance in order to satisfy all of humanity. Proof of that is that the granaries of the planet are full, and many nations, for economic reasons, subsidize farmers in order that they leave their fields to lie fallow. What happens when the countries that send humanitarian aid to mitigate the hunger of a nation? Generally, a great part of that aid is appropriated by the leaders of those poor nations, insensitive to the needs of their people. And then, isn't it true that this poverty and hunger is usually a result of ignorance of couples that barely can make a living, and decide to have a big family, condemning these children to a life of hunger, ignorance and suffering?

This is one facet, but fortunately there is another, for it is evident that mankind does not remain indifferent to the disasters that sporadically befall the planet, and it joins in sending aid to the victims. Some take pity while others remain indifferent. Not only that, there are also those that appropriate part of this aid to their own benefit. Duality in practice. Kindness and love on one side of the coin, and indifference and lack of love on the other. Again, human justice and injustice, not Divine.

But is it not an injustice that some are born with defects, paralysis, deformations, deafness, or with other physical deficiencies that keep them from enjoying a full life? What percentage of these defective births is caused by the parents? Drug addiction, alcoholism, violence and other vices can produce these defects. Also, humanity is exposed to the harmful chemicals of polluting industries due to the irresponsibility and voraciousness of their leaders or owners, or to noxious pharmaceutical drugs sold without exhaustive study. All this causes illnesses or serious mutations that undermine health or cause the death of millions; or the birth of babies that are condemned to AIDS by their infected parents. These are human errors that have nothing to do with the justice of God.

It would be absurd to think that God is unfair because Albert Einstein could discover the law of relativity and that I was not granted that gift. Such a comparison would not only be absurd, but stupid. Einstein's mind possessed the capacity to understand the workings of that revolutionary theory (MINE DID NOT), which he received as a spark from the universal mind, a gift transmitted to humanity by just one man whose publication of his theories opened up an enormous window on the advancement of science and on the intelligence of man.

Why should I complain that musical talent has been granted to so many, and the gift of genius to others, and not to me? Thank God that He has bestowed upon many the capacity of composing and interpreting music so that we may all enjoy it. It is a gift to humanity that makes the chords of our sensibility vibrate from happiness, including recollection and rapture.

It is clear that the Creator has taken care that the entire gamut of capabilities necessary to health and well being of humanity for the development of science and technology be provided and that, moreover, the most talented are those in charge of this undertaking.

One should appreciate our talents, and above all, appreciate the talents of others who, by broadening knowledge, make man's life richer and more pleasurable.

But why those differences in the intellect and abilities of people?

It is important to seek a reasoning that can convince us: could it be that those gifts are dealt out in a sort of lottery before birth? To be subject to chance in the distribution of gifts is unacceptable. It is as though marks would be given out as in a raffle at the end of courses at the university without considering the merit of those that made every effort in learning and understanding the lessons.

How is this evolution possible if we accept the concept that there is only one life in which the spirit can forge its eternal destiny? We have to reject this concept, since it does not clear up the differences in aptitudes and levels of intelligence in mankind. It leaves the Creator's work incomplete. It denies the evolution of the spirit, in spite of the clarity of the evolution of matter.

In order for the spirit to evolve it is necessary that it experience a number of lives, and through them, evolve as much in the degree of intelligence as in the ability to amplify its gifts and talents. And undoubtedly it is those that dedicate themselves with enthusiasm, devotion, and passion that get ahead much farther and faster. Goodness! This sounds good, but on accepting this as true, we have no other alternative but to suspect that reincarnation is part of the Divine plan.

To me, Divine justice is to be understood in another way. God does not punish. Each one of us is responsible for the evolution of his spirit, for his conscience, and his intellect. There exist laws of behavior imprinted on our conscience that we know we must respect. Each one, in accordance with its actions, makes himself deserving of reward or punishment. I insist: God does not punish, it is you who has punished yourself, and you should reap what you have sown. Indolence, greed, indifference to the pain of others, irresponsibility toward those near you, misuse of gifts that were granted you for your benefit and those close to you, deceit, hypocrisy, envy, arrogance, abuse of force, of power, murder and all sorts of harmful attitudes toward your fellow man. These actions will make of your next life an unpleasant experience, or perhaps full of suffering, according to the extent of your faults. Is it not more reasonable to think that it is how it should be, that God does not intervene, or judge, because it is unnecessary?

His laws are simply applied and therefore we are our own judges, because spiritually we clearly realize the errors we have committed.

If God has given us the liberty of free will, it is evident that he doesn't want us to be His puppets. I am convinced that He wants us to be the masters of our life; to reject the manipulation of those that pretend to impose on us their truth as the only truth we should believe in. We are free to pursue our own truth and forge our own convictions with integrity, with respect towards the ideas forged by others, but never, ever let your mind be incarcerated by those that pretend to possess the only truth.

If you do not believe in my truth, fine, search for yours. We have the right to disagree.

CHAPTER TEN

FRAGMENTS

When a member of a family commits a crime it becomes a stigma on the rest of the family. Is that not unfair? Well, it has been demonstrated that because some priests have sexually abused minors, it is thought that the rest have as well and this is equally unfair. A priest friend of mine, a worthy representative of Christ, whom I greatly respect, told me that he was walking along the streets of Queretaro with a fellow priest when a boy approached to greet them. To his surprise the boy's father caught up with him and ordered: do not touch the priests. It was an experience that deeply affected them. It is cruel to generalize unfairly, condemning all because of a few.

It is a shame to verify that the abuse of minors is a reprehensible and sickly practice that is prevalent in all strata of society. A criminal act. But how can he who takes vows of chastity, becomes a priest, and with impunity sexually abuses minors, betraying the church of Christ be described? And his superiors, who in order to avoid scandal, cover their crime? It is important to recognize that man is fallible, that he can yield to all types of temptation - and that includes all of humanity - and therefore it should not surprise us that some priests give in to the same reprehensible conduct, for they too, because of their human nature, are liable to succumb to baser instincts. In no way does that tarnish the image of the church. Why hide it? The law should simply be applied, as it would be to any criminal, without fear of scandal or hypocrisy. More damage is done to the image of the clergy when the faithful discover that these offenses are being covered up. And above all, what devastating effect it must produce on those that have heard the call of this vocation and have faithfully carried out the message of Christ, when they learn of these abuses that the hierarchy has covered up. That indeed damages the credibility of the ecclesiastic institution.

WHY DID THE ROMAN CHURCH DECIDE THAT PRIESTS COULD NOT MARRY?

The first reason is of economic origin for, in not possessing a wife and descendants, it would then be only the church who would inherit the priests' properties. The second reason deals with the difficulties of a married man to devote himself totally to his parishioners; otherwise, he would have to also face domestic problems which would affect dedication to his pastoral duties. This last one is a loose hypothesis that unfortunately has not been carried out much, because celibacy has not proven to be effective for many, for in spite of not being married, priests still neglect their pastoral duties, and since they are human beings, as is the laity, they take advantage of the opportunity to lay with women without feeling guilty or responsible. The flesh is weak. Would the laws of God not be followed more closely if they were to marry? Much of perverse sexual conduct would be avoided.

There is no doubt that some, through constant effort in a bloody battle against their own sexuality, have maintained their vows of chastity, but it would be naive to think that the majority have adhered to it. I repeat – these are laws that go against human nature. Whoever has the will and the strength of character, and is convinced that this makes him feel more Christian, then good for him, but to make general a prohibition of this sort, and insist that it be observed, only leads to deceit and hypocrisy.

Why not recognize that we humans are weak, that it is difficult for us to free ourselves from our passions, and that we succumb easily to temptation? Why the deception when truth is what liberates us?

I quote from Margaret Starbird's book, *The Lost Legacy of Mary Magdalene*.

Why was the Catholic Church so intent in demanding lifetime vows of celibacy from those aspiring to the priesthood? At the beginning, priests were married men. Peter had a mother-in-law, and Paul said that Jesus' brothers and the rest of the apostles travelled with their "sisters" (women), 1 Cor. 9, 4. Among the primitive Christians, the model was equality among the sexes and shared administration, as I understand it, based on the example of Mary Magdalene, an important figure of the community. Recent investigations by the Catholic theologian and arqueologist Dorothy Irvin contribute clear pictorial proof of women dressed in priestly attire, accompanied by epithets alluding to their administrative role, in which some were named bishops. Women were excluded after 494 in a decree by Pope Gelasius in which it was prohibited that they be ordained priests.

But according to the tradition of primitive Christianity, priests could marry. The movement of opposition to this intensified toward the end of the XIth century, ending in 1095 with the prohibition by Urban II of ordaining those married. (It is clear that this decision took more than one thousand years in expressing the rulings of the church, an example that demonstrates the handling of catholic concepts throughout time)

By a later decree during the reign of Pope Innocent II, married priests were forced to separate from their wives and children. The reason publicly given as an explanation of the new requirement for the priesthood was that the church wanted to ensure that its properties would remain in the hands of the hierarchy and not be inherited by the children of the priests. Nevertheless, this papal decision covered up the conviction that, in order to consolidate the power of the church, it was necessary to separate the priests from the influence of their wives.

A public statement by Pope Innocent II indicated this by saying that the church could not escape from the clutches of the laity if the priests did not escape from those of their wives. End of quote.

Pope Urban's decision to prohibit the married from being ordained seems a bit drastic to me, but cannot be reproached for they were not yet priests.

The decision of Innocent II is worthy of reproach for it requires that the priests already married abandon their wives and children. Is it not said that what God joins together may not be put asunder by man? What is Christian about a pope who by decree destroys the concept of marriage and leaves the families of those priests in need? For power and money?

There are those that believe that once the material body dies, the Creator grants a glorious different body to the spirit that has transcended material existence: free of earthly needs, free of any ties and suffering, flooded with a sensation of peace and happiness, enjoying absolute liberty, able to move anywhere in an instant by mere wish, able to discover the wonders of creation, and learning and laboring in the works of the Creator. What a marvelous hypotheses. Could they be right? I believe so, for this would certainly give us a possibility of eternal happiness.

When a body dies, what is customarily said is "rest in peace". Please, is it not better to ask that peace be reached? Why ask that it go into a corner to rest in peace if it is not tired? It is the body that was tired, exhausted, useless and finally rests in peace on death, as it is freed from all the pain, suffering, and pressures of life. But the spirit is set free and continues on; I should suppose that it will be happy to participate in the work of the Creator, to enjoy being useful, and delight in new experiences.

Baptism symbolically welcomes you into the Christian faith; I don't understand that a newborn is cleansed of sin when none has yet been committed. Or perhaps it means that God grants advance forgiveness of the mistakes that the baby could make during his lifetime and, on dying, his spirit would go directly to heaven as a result of said divine forgiveness. In this case, the concept of purgatory or a fearful hell would become unnecessary. It could easily be argued that it is original sin that is being cleansed. What sin? Who sinned and when? It has been said that Adam and Eve, figures of the imagination who never existed, ate an apple, because Eve tempted Adam to do so. I suppose they referred to the sex act. Here the tendency to make sex a sin is obvious, and so the good male chauvinists blamed Eve, when it would have been normal for the man, he of the testosterone, to be the one to tempt the woman. And to further denigrate women, they said that God created Eve from Adam's rib. Can they have been so blind as to not have seen that life is sown in a woman's womb?

Later this narrative was changed: Now what was eaten was the fruit of knowledge. As I have said before, knowledge is not eaten, but is a gift granted to us by the Creator. It also entails the capacity to act in good faith or bad, to love or to hate, and this liberty was the curse of humanity's expulsion from Paradise. This knowledge, misused, enables us to experience hate, envy, resentment, jealousy, voraciousness, and all those negative attitudes that can lead man to a living hell. But they cannot be cleansed; they should be struggled against during a lifetime, to be overcome by goodness and love.

But why do I dare doubt what is said in the book of Genesis regarding the myth of Adam and Eve? First of all, they tell us that man was created by God six thousand years ago. I accept that it occurred to them to say so at that time for they had no idea then of the orderly process of creation, and they had to account for it in a literary manner, with the purpose of explaining the inexplicable even to them. But in the midst of the twenty-first century that assertion is untenable, because scientists have discovered remains of Homo sapiens in Africa that date back to one hundred thousand years or more. This proves that man was not created six thousand years ago and shatters the concept of the Garden of Eden and the famous tree of life, guarded by cherubs with swords of fire.

The life of humanity does not originate from the molding of clay. It is a result of genetic programming that had its beginnings once the earth's environment became suitable for bacteria to develop. Humanity is the culmination of that inexplicable and miraculous genetic programming.

As an adolescent, I did not understand how a couple, theoretically created by a magical process could be the precursor of all humanity. A man and a woman mate and have two sons, Cain and Abel. Cain slays Abel with the jaw of a donkey. For goodness sake! Where did that donkey's jaw come from? It would have been more practical to have killed him with a heavy stone. Consequently, to replace poor Abel, Seth was conceived. Thus, humanity comes from incest in a foursome: Mother with son, father with wife and then, brothers with sisters, and fathers with daughters. For how many future generations must the genetic defects of this untenable experiment accumulate before they are buried and wiped out?

Adam and Eve is a myth but the effectiveness of brain-washing doesn't surprise me.

To delve further, we have the myth of Noah. God was angry with the behavior of humanity and told Noah that He was going to end it all, but since Noah was the only righteous man there, he would be saved together with his family. Noah begged the Creator for forgiveness, but His decision was final. Noah then had to build an ark to hold a pair of each animal species, as it was going to rain 40 days and 40 nights, until the waters covered the highest mountain on earth.

So Noah and his family began to build the ark and to capture a pair of each animal species.

Finally, the Creator told him that it was time to board the ark, and it started to rain during 40 days and 40 nights, until the last mountaintop on earth was covered.

Now, let's analyze the absurdity of this myth:

Where did the water come from to cover the whole planet – all of the earth's surface - with nine thousand meters more of water? We know that if all of the polar icecaps were to melt, the ocean level would rise approximately three hundred meters.

When the deluge ended, where did all that water go to for the earth to dry out?

The work of capturing pairs of animals in Noah's surroundings must have been arduous, and ultimately futile, because infinity of species inhabiting the rest of the planet was theoretically eliminated from the face of the earth by that deluge.

I can't imagine Noah roaming the earth to save species from places he did not know of or even knew existed.

It is then said that since all of humanity had perished in that deluge, Noah became the new Adam, that again, from an incestuous family, the new human race arose: White, black, yellow, Eskimo, dark-skinned, and red-skinned?

How absurd.

REFLECTIONS OF A BELIEVER

Even non-sapiens animals somehow know that incest is wrong and try to expel the males sexually mature from the pack during mating season. A good example of this is the behavior of elephants.

The females that have born male elephants chase them from the pack. How do they know that incest is wrong? It must surely be a part of their genes, or perhaps they are more intelligent than we believe them to be.

There is no reason for the church to be unaware of modern scientific discoveries for it to sustain erroneous beliefs today.

It would be the same as believing that the earth is the center of the universe and also, horrors, that it is flat, just because the church defended that thesis at the time of the Dark Ages. Of course, no one would dare to doubt now that the earth is just one of any number of planets in the universe, and that it is not, nor ever was, flat.

Now to the figure of Moses, with all due respect.

It is said that Moses climbed Mount Sinai for 40 days and 40 nights while God, seated on his gold throne amidst the clouds, dictated the tablets of the law.

I only ask: Did almighty and omniscient God need 40 days and 40 nights to dictate those laws inspired by Moses, laws that to me are really rules of simple ethics that any person with a good mind could have arrived to the same conclusion. Rules to promote respect to avoid misbehavior.

Does the Creator need a golden throne when He has everything?

I believe that the Creator's only wish is that we be happy, honorable, and as a consequence, full of love.

THE PACIENCE OF JOB

I can't believe that the omniscient God would wager with the Evil One for the love of Job, and as loving as He is, would make Job suffer all kinds of calamities to demonstrate his unswerving faith when He already knew the outcome.

As I see it, a religion cannot endure if based partially on true history but mainly on myths fabricated by man over the centuries.

All religions declare the same truth: Love and respect for their fellow man, but all have their weaknesses when claiming they possess the absolute truth and impose blind acceptance upon believers. They are institutions comprised of human beings who are preaching is the same and whose real and general purpose is to subject the human mind to ideas that allow religions to gain power and money by means of threats of damnation of those who do not blindly accept precepts declared to be of divine inspiration.

Not only is this control directed to the minds of the secular, but to those aspiring to the priesthood, to the most innocent and believing; the followers of lesser hierarchy are indoctrinated in such a manner that they believe in the threats of damnation should they dare to doubt the warped concepts of church leaders.

Personally, I am not affected by unbelievable myths – they seem entertaining and implausible to me. We should have the analytical capacity of discovering what our faith is based on, and not allow ourselves to be taken in by the church and its exclusive claim to divine inspiration. We all have access to God's inspiration. At some moment in our lives, we have all experienced a spark of that inspiration, albeit unconsciously.

There are those who think that once the body dies, the spirit remains prowling among its loved ones and perhaps may even give advice to one or some of them. Sounds good. I suspect that this may be so. That after some time, it passes on to a plane to which it belongs in the spiritual world, but also, it may be that it is permitted to return to visit its loved ones while awaiting the moment it must follow the evolving path. In what manner or on what plane will it continue to develop? How? Neither of us knows. We can only express a hypothesis that cannot be proven.

What beautiful cathedrals have been built over the centuries. Real jewels of great ostentation, decorated with paintings and sculpture by the geniuses of the Renaissance, inspired by Christian faith. But I have a doubt. Was it Christ's intention, in his message of humbleness the reason why those luxurious cathedrals were built in His name? Would it be pious to accumulate fabulous treasures in jewels, works of art and gold, while watching the needy die of cold or hunger?

Surely the blood spilled during the French revolution would have been avoided if the nobility and the clergy would have taken pity on the starving masses.

A divorced person is not allowed to receive communion but it is not denied to a murderer or child molester. It is unbelievable that divorce gets a harsher punishment than murder or sexual child abuse. Anyone with a little bit of mental awareness (not much is needed) can notice the absurdity, unfairness, and inconsistency of this mandate which fortunately many more open-minded priests ignore.

The Sanhedrin, the priest leadership, Caiaphas, Anas, and especially the Pharisee brought about the crucifixion of Christ; for they feared that His doctrine could destabilize their position of power and riches. They crucified an innocent man to protect their status. It was a handful of men who were guilty of this atrocity. Why condemn all, for the criminal dees of a few?

Jesus and his followers were Jewish. Christianity was born, took root in the beginning, among Jewish people.

This one man has had more influence on mankind than that of all of the kings, generals and philosophers. Altogether, they have not left an imprint so deep as that of Jesus Christ two thousand years ago. It is a phenomenon that ratifies the greatness of Christ, enduring and strengthening over the centuries in spite of the sins committed through the centuries in the name of God.

Whoever may be so innocent as to think that by just wearing a cassock, the purple, the red, or the canopy guarantees that the priests are a paragon of virtues, was unpleasantly surprised to know that many of them have behaved over the centuries as true anti-Christians, committing sins of all kinds of colors and flavors. History is there to prove it. All are human beings and therefore prone to succumbing to passion.

It is dangerous to oppose the hierarchies of powerful men, which is why Socrates was forced to drink hemlock because he dared to propose a philosophy similar to that of Christ.

OUR RIGHTS?

We undoubtedly have rights:

The right to freedom. But this can be lost when a crime is committed that legally justifies the imprisonment of the criminal.

The right to seek happiness. But no one has explained to us how to achieve it.

The right to brotherhood. A nice concept, but in order to fulfill it we should include consideration, respect, generosity, benevolence, solidarity, and all those other concepts we wish to add. And reality has shown us that when we only consider our rights, we inevitably fall into selfishness.

We find in the New Testament that Jesus, on preaching, did not speak to us of rights, but rather of obligations. Why? Because that is the way to respect the rights of others. Do not do unto others what you would not like them to do unto you. That is a mandate that covers the rights of both sides.

Love your neighbor as yourself. That is an objective to be reached and on doing so, offers us a feeling of spiritual peace that converts into a reward for the soul, approaching happiness, for it liberates us from harmful passions.

If we focus on fulfilling our obligations, we would obtain those rights as a consequence.

The teachings of Jesus are of immense wisdom; if mankind would limit itself to act in accordance with them, the planet would become a true paradise.

CHAPTER ELEVEN

JESUS CHRIST AND HIS MESSAGE

Many testimonies have been written about Him where we are told of His sermons, His parables, and His miracles, but very little do we know about the man Himself. How was His character? What did He like to do when not preaching? We know nothing in this regard and because of this, on missing this important information, we imagine Him to be a serious person, distant, and deep in thought, denying Himself the pleasure of enjoying the fruits of life in the flesh.

I cannot picture him that way. He must have been a Being of many aspects, friendly, cheerful, who knew how to enjoy the good things in life, who was deeply moved by human pain; at the same time, He should have been of strong character, well composed when the occasion called for it. What better proof of that than to have sought to be crucified. And why? Not to wash and forgive the sins of humanity with His blood, for how many oceans of it would have to overflow to achieve that objective?

Are we to understand His sacrifice as something indispensable to demonstrate His love for mankind, as it was necessary to cement His message of salvation that would remain written with indelible words in the heart of humanity? I believe SO. On the contrary, how would

His message would have transcended without having proven His immortality?

He knew that it was necessary to live through that ordeal in order to leave a deep imprint of His mission on earth and at the same time, demonstrate His immortality. This achievement is described to us in the gospels for it was said that Jesus appeared before the apostles after the crucifixion in a body they did not recognize, that it was not the same as that of Jesus but rather the divine body of Jesus Christ.

With respect to what is written, later comes the historically-proven miracle of when He gave them the enlightenment on granting them the Holy Spirit, they suddenly understood their calling, and left to preach His word to the four cardinal points convinced of their own immortality. Just a few fishermen, surely illiterate, that had loved but did not understand Him, set out to confidently preach, without fear, probably in many languages? Is not this a true miracle, proven by the historical tales of the work of the apostles?

Therefore, it is my understanding that this was the objective of Christ on seeking and accepting this agony.

I refuse to accept the concept that God sent His son to suffer on the cross. This is a contradiction, for it is assured that God is love. By saying that He is capable of sending His son so that, as a result of His suffering, He could forgive the sins of humanity, is an offense to a loving God, who, on being Almighty, can forgive without the need of that cruel mandate.

Jesus was also a man and as such, had the right to use his free will.

Would it be acceptable to think that He decided to carry on with what was written necessary, so that His message would not be lost in the mist of time? Supposedly that was so.

That Christ came to bring us salvation is true, but not as a result of His sacrifice. He came to bring us, through His preaching, a message of a deep philosophy of love, where He shows us the way to defeat evilness, the certainty that God loves us, and the immortality of the spirit, and therefore to not believe in a God capable of being cruel and righteous, but in a fair and loving God. Thus, the basic content of His message was: love God above all, and your neighbor as yourself, as love is the sentiment that can CURE and through it, save our soul. As simple as that. There is no need to add any more baroque concepts that only confuse the believer.

As Saint Augustine said: (confessions) LOVE and do whatever you want.

If Jesus had been crucified before performing the miracles attributed to Him, and He had abstained from making His profound and marvelous sermon, what significance would his crucifixion have had? Who would have cared, for thousands were crucified in those days? Undoubtedly his family and friends, and no one else. Therefore, what was truly striking about the life of Jesus was His miracles, His humanitarian concepts of a very profound philosophy, and His message of love.

Why represent Him as a physical wreck hanging from a cross?

The cross is a belated symbol of Christianity for it was originally identified with the figure of a fish. Later, it was represented by the figure of a cross, and finally the figure of a crucified Christ was added. What is the point of representing the body of Jesus in that state? A day's suffering is more significant that His whole life? Does this not lead to the erroneous idea that to flagellate the body, a pointless masochism, is the way to please God? How can we think that we please God by martyrizing the marvelous body He has endowed us with?

I insist – as I see it – that Christ sought crucifixion because it was a way to show His immortality and cement His work on earth in our hearts. Undoubtedly, it was a very bitter blow, for He did not do it for the pleasure of the pain; but that was the savage manner of the times and how those considered criminals were punished. He had no other alternative but to achieve his objective. He did not show us that one should flagellate oneself or suffer in order to be a good Christian; that is an erroneous interpretation that provokes masochism, of no benefit to anyone, and seriously harms those who are confused by this belief and resort to torture. Totally to the contrary: He came to teach us how to be happy, and live with joy on possessing the capacity to love and be loved.

We have learned that Pope Benedict XVI on February 10, 2008, at the Vatican, explains what it signifies to enter into Lent, and in the last paragraph says: the message that the Virgin still conveys in Lourdes reminds us of the words that Jesus pronounced on starting His mission and that we hear often in these days of Lent: "Convert and believe in the gospel", pray and make penitence.

Make penitence. What kind of penitence? Why does the church still insist that penitence must be made? What benefit can mortifying you and making penitence by mandate bring to you or your neighbor, against your will and of your own will? Did Jesus ask anyone to make penitence? He asked that they repent and sin no more.

If you pray fervently, it gives you peace, but if you pray to fulfill penitence, you are on the edge of emptiness.

Whatever is done with love, however difficult it may be, is not penitence but a pleasure, and you would have done a good deed to your neighbor.

On entering Lent we should remember and feel in our hearts the marvelous message of Jesus.

OPEN YOUR HEARTS AND FEEL COMPASSIONET AND HELP THOSE WHO SUFFER. This would make a more just message of the Savior, whose objective was not to make us suffer; all to the contrary - as I understand it - for by following His philosophy it would allow us to obtain happiness and on doing so, add our grain of sand by helping our neighbor to attain it as well.

It is said that Judas betrayed Jesus. If He was not aware of this, then there is no doubt of the betrayal. But it also said that Jesus knew of it. It would have been logical then for Him to leave to avoid being captured; nevertheless, He remained. It is also said that He told Judas: go and do what you have to do. That is clear to me that there was no betrayal at all, for the consent of Jesus is obvious. Why erroneously describe Judas as a traitor? If all this is true, it can be affirmed that He wanted to go through that torture, and therefore, entrusted Judas to give Him up. It is possible to think that facts were manipulated to foment anti-Semitism, pointing to a Jew in particular as the traitor that caused the death of Jesus. Did not Jesus and His apostles belong to the Jewish community? Paul of Tarsus was a citizen of Rome but he was also a Jew. If what is written is true, then accusing Judas as a traitor is illogical and contradictory to the facts.

That Christ said: he who is not with Me is against Me. I do not take this as a threat, but rather as - he who does not follow My teachings, he who does not heed My message (where it is clear that the only way is love), he who commits only evil, cannot achieve the rewards of the righteous.

This is valid for all of mankind, even those professing a different religion, as long as their conduct is that of goodness and love.

It is written in the Lord's Prayer: forgive our offenses as we forgive those who have offended us. This is valid if we forgive those who have offended us. If we do not know how to forgive, how can we expect to be forgiven?

Thy will be done on earth as it is in heaven. To me, this is a concept that cannot be questioned. But how could we explain that humanity does whatever it wants and at its will? Exactly, for it is the will of the Creator that this is so, He who granted us the liberty of free will.

There are those who insist that the body of Jesus rose after crucifixion, in spite of the centurion's spear piercing His heart, perhaps as an act of pity, for it avoided that His legs would eventually be broken, as was done in those days, to increase the pain of the crucified in their terrible agony. Despite the fact that surely many hours had passed before His body was laid in the tomb, the nerve cells of the brain had obviously died, and the decomposition of the flesh begun. In spite of that, there are those who sustain that the body rose from the dead. And why would they think that? Because they believe if God was capable of creating everything, He had the power to do this simple feat.

My belief is that God created His laws, and it may be deducted that among them the resurrection of a decomposing body is not one. It is logical to think that if this were possible within His laws, then it would not have been necessary to use the womb of the Virgin Mary for the gestation of the body of Jesus.

Other theologians think the opposite: it was Jesus Christ who appeared after the death of the physical body, in his divine and immortal body, which, as such, could not have died. That could have been done without breaking any laws of the Creator. Do we dare to know all of His laws? Of course not. But we can deduct, just by observing the development of nature, those which are not permitted by His laws to happen.

In the Old Testament it is believed that God created Adam molding him from clay then giving him life with his divine breath. That is a nice way of explaining how mankind was born; in those days little was known of the laws of nature, and what better way to explain them than in a literary manner. That was acceptable for the times, but currently we know that in order for humanity to appear, a process of thousands of millions of years of evolution was needed, by means of genetic programming in accordance with the earth's environment had to be carried out. This leads me to believe that within His laws of nature nor the molding of bodies from clay and giving them life, nor bringing a decomposing body back to life is contemplated.

After centuries and centuries of thoughtful theological study, the resurrection of the body of Jesus is still not agreed upon; nevertheless we have always been assured that His body arose from the dead. How can this be, when there are differing opinions within the church?

I would suppose that Christ had, with the crucifixion, ended his mission for which it was necessary to occupy a body. Therefore, I think that the body was no longer useful to Him. Why insist in affirming that His body rose from the dead when in the scriptures it is said that Christ appeared before his apostles in a body they did not recognize? Does not that clearly indicate to us that the body of Jesus did not resurrect? In what body did he appear? If what the scriptures tell us is correct, it was in his divine body, not that of Jesus.

It is said that Jesus stated: of the weak (or poor) of spirit will be the kingdom of heaven. It can be thought that this is mistakenly interpreted in the translation of this message. Why condemn the strong spirits that, with their strength, are those in charge of getting ahead in the progress of humanity? I think that it should be interpreted as: of the tender of heart will be the kingdom of heaven - to show compassion, love, and forgiveness for your fellow human being. I feel that this is enough.

What can be thought of those who take the vows of poverty and cover themselves in gold?

Of the poor will be the kingdom of heaven. Here appears another possibility of man's manipulation for it is a manner of controlling the poor with the promise that they will enter the kingdom of heaven if they obediently accept their situation.

It is questionable when the church describes a poor person as someone lacking in economic funds; true poverty should be described as lacking in love. Whoever is not nourished by love is truly poor, for happiness is beyond his reach.

If someone hits you on the right cheek, offer him the left as well.

If someone assaults you, or puts your life in danger, of course you should defend yourself, for no one has the right to harm your body, the temple of God.

If someone offends you, or does you harm, offering the other cheek, in this case, means to return the offense by doing a good deed. This is an attitude that will surely induce the offender to be ashamed and apologize, bringing about a friendship instead of an unnecessary enmity.

Love your enemies, for if you only love whoever loves you, what merit is that? Difficult, right? But, does not this liberate you from your passions, your resentments, and even hate?

Does not hate, resentment or envy become a hell making you ill and unable to live in peace? I understand that as hard and difficult it may be, it is the only way to be free from the burden of hate and resentment, by saying love your enemies. Love allows you to forgive and frees your soul of all resentment, bringing harmony to your life and the peace of mind that happiness provides.

In the creed of the apostles it is said that Jesus was crucified, died, and buried, that He descended to hell, and on the third day rose from the dead. How may that be interpreted? If it is clarified that Christ descended in spirit then we may conclude that He did not die, for I repeat, his body, that of Jesus, was dead, and could not have descended or ascended anywhere. It sounds better to say that he descended in spirit; since our belief is that the spirit is immortal, and being so, it is inacceptable to say that he died, and since he is immortal, it is improper to say that he resurrected, since he did not die.

REFLECTIONS OF A BELIEVER

Now then, it is said He descended to hell. It is important that it be explained to us where hell is, and why Christ went to such an inexistent place.

There is confusion regarding hell. First we are told that it is a terrifying place where the evil minded are destined to suffer for all of eternity. Later, it is believed that it is not a place but a state of the spirit that suffers for its sins, and now we have just learned that Pope Benedict XVI assured that it does exist as a place, and that it is occupied. I confess that this difference of opinions within the same church confuses me, and awakens my incredulity. How is it possible to assure its existence when it is only a hypothesis that is not humanly possible to prove? Why would the Pope have wanted to firmly assure us that hell exists? Then we are told that we are to have different interpretations of what the Pope said. What did he mean?

On reading the book, *Jesus of Nazareth*, written by Pope Benedict XVI, page 41, I found a quote on the baptism of Jesus, and was uncertain if it was only a quotation, or rather an affirmation that recognizes the veracity of its content. I do not know, but if I have to literally interpret what is stated there, I cannot avoid disagreeing.

I quote: through its liturgy and theology of the icon, the eastern church has developed and gone into depth about this way of understanding the baptism of Jesus.

The iconography picks up on these similarities. The icon of the baptism of Jesus shows water as a liquid tomb in a dark cave that at the same time is the representation of Hades and hell. Jesus descending to this liquid tomb, to this hell that envelops him, is the representation of going to hell. (The entrance and exit of the water are a representation of descending to hell and the resurrection).

On describing the water like a liquid tomb, in a dark cave, that at the same time represents hell, appears to me, with all due respect, like wanting to explain, in the most implausible manner, the concept of hell, especially when water symbolizes cleanliness, is used for the sacrament of baptism, and is also an indispensable element for the development of life.

Now then, if it is affirmed that hell is a place where there is fire, it is evident that it cannot be dark, and by being surrounded by water, this would inevitably be boiling and vaporizing constantly. I must confess that this reference seriously confuses me.

It is also thought that on descending to hell, He expelled the devil from there after fighting and defeating him. So this place disappears, it is no longer the domain of evil. Hell disappears, but, in spite of all, evil still prowls around humanity.

It is logical to deduct that if the visit to hell was made by Jesus when he was baptized, and He expelled Satan from that place, we must recognize that after the crucifixion, He did not descend to hell, for this hypothetical place no longer existed. Then it is said a new humanity and a new world arises from this. New? Reality has proven that evilness in mankind has not been eliminated, that everything is the same or worse, and that the terrible evildoing continues as it pleases.

As I understand it, it is evident that Christ did not come into our lives to fight against the devil and defeat it. This would make us erroneously suppose that evilness is an existing being, alive, that can be fought, when it is really only a symbol that describes evil. On affirming that He fought against evil and defeated it would be to accept that He failed in doing so, for He did not destroy human evilness.

I insist: He came to bring us a message of love, which is the formula for allaying the evilness in our life, but that effort is the responsibility of mankind, not of Christ. He showed us the way, but we are the ones with the option of following it or not, and therefore, the only ones responsible for our actions.

REFLECTIONS OF A BELIEVER

By eliminating by decrce the possibility of evilness, we would be destroying the concept of free will and denying humanity the possibility of choice, and the merit of its goodness.

That on being baptized Jesus He took on His shoulders the sins of mankind. Excuse me? All the sins of the past, present, and future?

How can we say that we love Him, yet calmly dump on Him the very sad task of taking on all of the sins of humanity? It is very easy to leave that task to Jesus. Why did the church insisted in menacing the believers with hell and purgatory, they also affirm that Jesus has taken on His shoulders all the sins of humanity?

One concept contradicts the other.

To my way of thinking that is an affirmation that confuses rather than clarifies. Jesus did not come to wash away our filth; he came to teach us how to do it ourselves, giving us the formula of behavior that, on following it, we would take over the washing, healing and saving of our souls, a formula of goodness and love. It is that simple. We are the ones who have to fight to allay evilness from our hearts.

Every one of us is responsible for his errors, and as I understand it, takes charge of our sins. It is clear that only he or she can purge them. How? I do not know. These are many hypotheses that are just that, for NO ONE can prove that any of them are true.

He rose from among the dead, went up to heaven, and is seated on the right hand of God the Father.

To be seated on the right hand of God the Father is an allegory that explains what the Christians perceive the magnitude and greatness of Christ, but He cannot be seated anywhere for it is evident that He is close to all of mankind.

REFLECTIONS OF A BELIEVER

Now then, to say that he rose to heaven would be appropriate for me to interpret as an evolution upward, toward a higher spiritual level, because how do we know where heaven is? Up, down, in any other cardinal point, everywhere, IN ANOTHER DIMENSION, or simply in the spirit of those who have been righteous, loving, kind-hearted, and deserving?

To state that He rose to heaven in body and soul confuses me greatly for if it is the physical body, of skin and bones that is referred to, it seems to me to be totally impractical, an unacceptable opinion. It was thought that heaven was to be found among the clouds. We would necessarily have to affirm that a body of perhaps eighty kilos, tied to earth by the force of gravity, could not ascend anywhere without something to propel it. It could probably be affirmed that God can do anything, but why would the Creator have bothered to magically place Jesus among the clouds when, in the first place, heaven is not found there, and if He were to place Him among or above the clouds, the body of Jesus would immediately freeze, He would asphyxiate for lack of oxygen, and inevitably die.

Jesus spoke to us of eternal life, and our faith is based on the immortality of the BEING found in that disposable body which, once deceased, rots and recycles into nature. Therefore, taking into consideration our faith, or at least mine, it is the Divine body, spiritual, immortal, in which Jesus Christ moves wherever and whenever He pleases in complete freedom.

THE MYSTICS BELIEVE THAT THERE ARE SEVEN PLANES OF SPIRITUAL EXISTENCE (The mystic of Islam speaks of seven circles and Saint Teresa of Jesus of seven dwellings in Christianity). And on the death of the body, the spirit occupies the corresponding plane in accordance with its evolution toward goodness and love. If that be so, Christ is above these.

Jesus Christ is God?

He never said that he was God. He spoke of his Father; therefore he is the Son of God. Are we not all sons of God? If that be so, how can we understand Christ if we call him the only son of God?

REFLECTIONS OF A BELIEVER

I want to make it clear that I am not only a believer but convinced of the existence and immortality of Christ. That He is here among us and that eventually He reveals himself to some. That He was is and will be. But it is my understanding that God is universal, or rather, part of all of the universe and that this is of an immensity that covers hundreds of thousands of millions of galaxies; and our marvelous planet appears as a grain of sand in all that vastness, for which we cannot place the Creator in a single planet, when innumerable planets exist in the universe. Therefore I believe that Christ is really the Son of God, a spirit of an evolution and very high hierarchy, which overshadows us. But we too are children of God in the process of evolution on an intellectual and spiritual scale.

Christ said: you too can accomplish what I have done. What did He mean by that? How may we interpret his words? Each of us who cares should seek an answer applicable to them.

It is clear to me that He tells us that our possibilities of spiritual evolution give us the ability to cure, both physically and emotionally; and what is more, that they are qualified as miracles (that really are not) for they become so thanks to the Divine laws and the true faith of the believer. Faith moves mountains, said Christ, according to what the gospels say, and this true faith can trigger a self-curative reaction in our organisms. Is not infinity of miraculous cures attributed to some saints as well?

Mankind would be chaos if hierarchies did not exist, and considering the concept as it is down, it is up, both should be similar. I believe that there also exist hierarchies in the spiritual world. This concept is dealt with by the Catholic church when it assures us that the angels, archangels, cherubs, etcetera exist in spirit. That allows me to think that Christ is a much higher hierarchy than those above but, may we also say that He is God of the universe?

According to the scriptures, the apostles, when they addressed Jesus, called him Rabi, not God Almighty. Santiago, who was said to be the brother of Jesus, and possibly the most loved, never referred to Him as God. There are those who think that after the death of Jesus, it was Santiago, not Peter, who was the true pillar of His philosophy, for he was the one who knew and understood Him the most. It is possible to deduce that it was Paul of Tarsus who promoted the idea of the Deification of Jesus.

In the trial before the crucifixion it is said that Jesus was asked if He was king, and He answered: you have said so, but My kingdom is not of this world. Christ is the eternal spiritual King of our world. But not a king in the human sense that requires submission to his will but rather a teaching king that guides souls in their evolution while seeking enlightenment.

If it is said that God sent Christ to suffer on the cross to cleanse the sins of humanity, is not a differentiation being made between God, who ordered, and Christ, who carried out those orders? Does this not confirm a difference in hierarchy between God the Creator and Jesus Christ?

Now then, I ask: who am I to dare question ancient concepts in time when it is supposed that the ecclesiastic hierarchy and its theologians are the masters of the truth?

It is simply because I am a believer that questions the machinated truths by means of the cerebration and convenience of men who have manipulated these truths at their whim, many of them with no foundation whatsoever. How many modifications have been made over the centuries, many of them with manipulative overtones, where it is clear that they have nothing to do with the Divine, but are rather very human?

Now then, it is stated that Christ is GOD OF THE UNIVERSE, THE CREATOR OF ALL THINGS. But as such, then we should recognize that it is He to which the Jews in the Old Testament refer to, leading us to the conclusion that there are more discrepancies to be taken into consideration.

That God said: Grow and multiply. As seen by the Roman Catholic church Christ approved chastity, that it was agreeable to God. Does that mean that God changed his mind? At a time of such loss of life? To what human mind did it occur inserting that idea into religion? An idea that is totally against human nature, where sex is described as something sinful, when in reality it is a wonderful of the gift from the Creator that ensures the continuity of life of perfect organisms that exist on this marvelous planet.

Vow of chastity? There must be some who fulfill it, but the great majority does not. Not only that - and I repeat - it has been discovered that some, enough, sexually abuse minors, a crime that at all costs has been covered up to not jeopardize the image of the church. Once made public, we are horrified, and how many believers awaken from their innocence on becoming aware of the hypocrisy and deceit of those who are supposed to represent God on earth? This not only harms the image of the church but also seriously affects the faithful, for it creates confusion and doubt with regard to trusting in the priests and their teachings.

Why that perturbed urge to convert sex into something sinful? Surely because it is thought that Jesus was chaste. I am not aware if there exists a passage in the gospels where mention is made of the chastity of Jesus, and I will not take the time to go over them because, to me, the concept of chastity refers to the purity of spirit, purity of heart, that avoids evil and is nourished with the love of neighbor - a being free of negative passions, who understands and forgives human weakness. That, to me, is true chastity and in that sense, Jesus was undeniably chaste.

Everything done with love cannot be sinful.

Can you consider an evil person chaste for having been able to contain and destroy the sexuality of his body?

If we have decided that He is God of the universe, the Creator of all things, why deny sexuality when it is an indispensable part of His own creation? In Genesis it states that God said: IT IS NOT GOOD THAT MAN SHOULD BE ALONE; I WILL MAKE SUITABLE HELP

REFLECTIONS OF A BELIEVER

FOR HIM (Gen.2, 18). Christ was made man in the body of Jesus, a body of flesh and bones, not an immaterial one, with all of the needs, pleasures and sufferings that that implied. Why do we wish to reject the good, the beauty of life, and accept only the suffering of the crucifixion? How selfish and sanctimonious we are!

What I feel very serious is the recognition that all the errors, hypocrisies, cruelties, and assassinations that have been committed throughout the centuries in the name of God, not only offend Christ, but the Creator of all things, the universal God. How is it possible to obtain forgiveness when God is offended in such a way?

That Pope John Paul II asked forgiveness for the errors of the church is a brave stance but it is evident that he could not modify the fundamental structure of the church, returning it to a true Christianity, legitimate, a mission, with humility, and with a true vocation of charity, compassion and service.

I recognize a great confusion by touching on these subjects of which we humans know little about, although some try to. I do not wish to offend the beliefs of others, but we all have a right to express our convictions, accepting that they could be wrong. As I have said, it is my truth, and I insist that Christ, for me, is the spiritual king of our planet, a spirit of great generosity – as I have clearly expressed – but He is not the Creator of all things, God of the universe. That is the truth as I see it. We have no idea of how God really is, we cannot identify Him as we would a person, but we can be certain that He is a irrefutable reality by just observing the inconceivable intelligence shown in His creation.

Christ is among us. His message of love was very clear; it is unnecessary to complicate it with concepts that only cloud what really should be transparent.

It is certain that we are all prisoners of the unnamed powers that manipulate us! (Wise words spoken by Pope Benedict XVI).

AMEN

CHAPTER TWELVE

A CONVERSATION WITH MY FRIEND FATHER JUAN

Juan, a priest friend of mine, once told me, convinced, that only through the church can God be reached.

That seemed to be an arrogant statement but I refrained from comment knowing that he had entered the seminary when he was only 11, and had undoubtedly been brain-washed with the anachronic concepts of that period, which did not allow questioning under threat of excommunication.

Tell me why I should entrust my soul to an institution whose hierarchies, especially, have committed crimes of every nature, and have sent the faithful to war to reconquer the Holy Land, under the supposed objective of recovering Jerusalem, which was never theirs. The real purpose was to conquer and annex the land and riches: An adventure in looting, rape and murder - IN THE NAME OF GOD?

The Pope guaranteed that all the sins of those who died in that adventure would be forgiven, a plenary indulgence. Where did the certainty of divine power come from that would authorize such a blood-letting, killing and more killing, in the name of God, breaking one of the most important commandments in the tablets of the law – THOU SHALL NOT KILL?

"It's true what you say, but it was at a turbulent time", and they were human beings after all.

True, you are right, but would it is acceptable to deceive the faithful over centuries and centuries, making them believe that churchmen are God's representatives on earth? Not only in those barbaric times were atrocities committed in the name of God. Later, the Inquisition was instituted to further throttle innocent believers and increases the church's dominion through fear; an act of absolute arrogance, for no one would be tolerated who doubted the truth of what was considered divine law. Whoever dared to express a different idea was condemned as a heretic.

Look, Victor, the Inquisition was really dedicated to defending those who were accused of heresy.

My good friend, how innocent you are! How can you believe that to be true?

You well know that in 1231 Pope Gregory IV instituted the Tribunal of the Inquisition and 21 years later, Pope Innocent IV AUTHORIZED TORTURE. How disgusting! With the methods of torture in use at that time, anyone would confess to anything. If it was declared that you came from Mars for purposes of corruption, you would accept it. If you were told that you had sex with a mule, you would accept that so they would stop torturing you. They would say yes to whatever occurred to their torturers. If I thought they were beasts, I would be offending the poor animals. If hell existed, the worst possible punishment there for their unlimited inhumanity wouldn't be enough. Who can think that those popes represented God? THEY WERE THE INCARNATION OF SATAN!

Some examples:

Savonarola, a monk of the Renaissance, was a man of science, burnt at the stake for his advanced scientific ideas that did not agree with those of the Church.

Joan of Arc became the scourge of the English, capable of inspiring the French troops to win repeated victories over the enemy. The French refused to lay down their arms. This caused a difficult political situation between France and England, so Joan of Arc fell into the hands of the Inquisition and was sentenced to death because she would not forsake her beliefs – she had had a divine vision. The verdict was HERESY, AND SHE WAS BURNT AT THE STAKE.

If a pope asserts that his decision came to him as a divine revelation and it should therefore be respected, he is not committing heresy. Joan of Arc was declared a heretic for maintaining that she had received a divine sign. Could it be that divine inspiration is exclusive to popes?

I don't wish to say more on this subject, for much has been written regarding the abuses of the (holy?) Inquisition, but for how many centuries did that dreadful tribunal last?

I insist – they were very strange times. Human errors, not divine.

Of course, but I can't accept that they excuse themselves from committing the atrocities of an institution whose true labor is simply to preach the Word of Jesus. Christianity is based on love. Man has converted love as a message of evil, deceit, and terror. That is unforgivable and needs immediate correction. The work of the church should be a missionary one. As I understand it, Jesus didn't require of the church hierarchy to be leaders of humanity involved in matters of no concern to them, and restricting believers' emotional freedom by rules of behavior to be obeyed under threat of damnation.

Because of our friendship, I have not referred to your statement that God may be reached only through the church. If that is what they taught you, I can understand that you believe this. I think though, and no offense meant, that you reach God through love, not through ecclesiastic institutions. You yourself have tried to justify the abuses and crimes committed by the church, arguing that they have been human errors. Right, but you can't convince me of the idea that only through the church may God be reached. History has shown the evilness and the hypocrisy of those arrogant churchmen who have tried to make us believe that they are God's representatives on earth.

Any human being, educated or not, wealthy or poor, who really understands Christ's message of love, whether priest or layman, can reach God without the intercession of church bureaucracy, providing their deeds warrant it.

A bit of analysis would reveal the great contradictions in the concepts of the church. We are told that God is love, but also that He has the power of condemning His children to eternal torment. If that were so, the loving God becomes an evil monster who takes pleasure in tormenting the weak that have erred in their behavior. Is it not an offense against a loving God to state that He can act perversely? Is it possible that those doctrinaires do not notice this aberration?

Victor, you are being cruel with the church. Things are changing. Little by little untenable concepts, such as the famous limbo, are being eliminated. It is a difficult process and all those errors can't be eradicated from one day to another; it would be too great a trauma for the faithful.

Things have changed because today you can't act in an openly criminal manner. The universal church now recognizes religious freedom. The concept that salvation of the soul is possible only through the Catholic Church no longer exists. It is evident that salvation or punishment depends on human conduct, not on how many times mass is heard or what religion is practiced. I am Christian by conviction, but respect the beliefs of other religions and think that Christ is present in all of humanity, for we are all children of God.

It is possible that eliminating erroneous concepts all at once could be traumatic, especially for fanatics, but we are in the twenty-first century now. Humanity is awakening from its intellectual lethargy, and it may be the moment to make these changes, since modern minds better understand that those concepts come from centuries past, when any barbaric practice could be imposed on the faithful without questioning. It would be a relief to the believer that those bothersome errors of the past be eliminated just like that; I'm sure that they would understand.

Victor, I respect what you think, for I cannot refute what you have said, as it has been corroborated by history, but we are all part of the church, and it is also true that many have unselfishly and lovingly dedicated themselves to helping their fellow man. You can't deny that. I insist that the church is an institution made up of men and women, humans after all, some of whom are liable to err and others of committing unforgivable and despicable actions; but on analyzing the good and the bad, it is evident that goodness far surpasses evil.

It is true that goodness wins over evil; if this were not so, humanity would not exist. I have never denied that there are many who behave in a Christian-like manner. They are the pillars that justify the existence of the church, that show us that they are capable of following the teachings of Jesus with true vocation for helping their fellow man. Nevertheless, you cannot deny them the right to condemn or feel anger toward those who so calmly betray the doctrines of Jesus.

Victor, what you say troubles me for I must admit that I agree with you. I fear it is very difficult, or even impossible, to correct this.

You should well know that. A complete collapse would be necessary to start again. That possibility doesn't exist. No one would meekly accept giving up power.

REFLECTIONS OF A BELIEVER

Juan, what do you think of the dogmas?

Victor, what do you think?

Regarding dogmas, I admit to not having delved much into this subject.

Perhaps there is a hidden interpretation that I am unaware of. But there is a dogma that surprises me, since it affirms the infallibility of the Pope in the exercise of his office.

Supposedly, the Pope is divine and infallible, when in reality he is human and as such cannot be infallible or perfect. Over centuries, the question of the infallibility of the Pope was discussed without reaching any definite agreement. Finally, in 1867, Pope Pius IX decided to raise this concept to dogma.

As I understand it, it was a decree where the arrogance of Pope Pius IX was clearly discernible. He finally imposed his will although he certainly must not have received much support from the curia. This is a dogma I cannot accept, and I suppose that if it were not that dogmas are inviolable, the church would then have ruled it out as inappropriate.

In 1950 the concept of the Assumption of Mary was made dogma of the church by Pope Pius XII. It states that the Virgin Mary rose to heaven in body and soul, and if this be true, I should not be condemned if I do not accept it. Why does that idea appear after two thousand years? It is madness to declare that she rose to heaven in body and soul.

It's unbelievable how the same church that speaks to us of the immortality of the soul, the true being that inhabits the mortal body out of necessity, then insists upon considering the body as necessary to life in the spiritual realm.

And it would then be interesting for the church to explain where this heaven can be found. It's obvious that it has no idea, and neither do

I, but I think that it is to be found in another – spiritual - dimension without the need of a cumbersome body that has fulfilled its earthly function as a vehicle where the soul experiences life in the flesh.

As to the rest of the dogmas, I recognize I am not qualified to give an opinion.

Do you mean that you have doubts?

Don't you?

My faith in God and Jesus Christ is unswerving. That's what is important to me.

Thanks, you have made your answer clear.

Victor, I haven't clarified anything; I just don't want to broach that subject.

I understand. How can concepts we can't prove be analyzed?

Victor, I want to be honest with you. There are some dogmas that are based on inspirations of theologians which make no sense to me. I tell you this and beg you not to tell anyone what I have said. My faith is basic: God, Jesus Christ, and eternal life. All the rest appear to be ornamental opinions that have muddled the meaning of the teachings of Jesus. I can't ignore the great errors of the heads of the church, nor can I pretend that man be perfect. We are besieged by temptations, some, as Diaz Mirón said, emerge from difficulties unruffled*, and others, perhaps many, can't avoid getting soiled; passion takes over and they get dirty. It would be utopian if all respected the restrictions of the Catholic religion - to affirm that many go against human nature is unavoidable.

I appreciate your sincerity. I understand that you felt Christ's calling, so much a basic part of your faith, while having to ignore the weaknesses of man, an understanding of which is essential for keeping the faith.

But tell me, why attribute divinity to the male, the Father, when I think that God is everything, Father and Mother?

All religions accept this.

So they say, but could you not think of the possibility that this is not so? If religions state that God created man in His own image, doesn't it make you wonder if women should not have the right to think that they were also created in His own image? And we can categorically affirm that what is feminine is a far more complex and important creation, for it is in the womb that the life of animals begins, both in rational beings as well as in those unable to reason. If we can believe in the apparitions of the Virgin, can we not attribute the Creator's female side to this phenomenon?

But Jesus Christ was a man.

What does that prove to me?

That God is manifested in the body of Jesus, and religion assures us that He was God, creator of all things.

I will repeat that I am convinced that Jesus Christ is a spirit of grandeur far beyond us. A messenger from the Supreme Being who came to bring us a clear and easily understood missive that specifically insists that the path to spiritual perfection, to happiness, is but one: Love.

Jesus, the anointed, the illuminated, He that could perform deeds that seem miraculous to us.

I believe in Jesus Christ, probably with more conviction than many, a spirit much more elevated than ours, and in our midst, guides us on the road toward spiritual fulfillment.

To me, Jesus Christ is not the creator of all things. I cannot believe that the God of the universe (where surely there are trillions of planets such as ours) came to occupy a body upon this, an insignificant – in relation to the whole universe – but wonderful planet to learn how whip-lashes, ridicule, taunting, and the suffering of a crucifixion feel.

I find that inconceivable.

Victor, I don't wish to continue talking on this subject. I confess that you have shaken me with your way of thinking; I know that you are convinced of its validity, and this is your right. I cannot agree with you because I think differently but I believe that neither you nor I can say that we possess the absolute truth. I respect your point of view in spite of differing with you.

My dear friend, I didn't mean to upset you. I apologize and am in agreement with what you said. Neither of us possesses the absolute truth; it would be most arrogant to assume that we do.

I'm curious, forgive my indiscretion: What induced you to enter the priesthood, some divine revelation? Or a vocation, an inexplicable conviction that it was your calling and you wanted to pursue it?

Your question is irrelevant; however, I will say that I have never had an experience of the great beyond. My vocation came from who knows where, but what is true is that it was what I wanted to do with my life; I felt it in the depths of my being. I can't explain it, but I never doubted that it was the path I should and wanted to travel.

Believe me, there is a reason for questioning you because my dream as an adolescent was to study organic chemistry, but since my father, whom I loved dearly, worked in the textile industry and wanted me to be a part of his business, I gladly studied business administration. On graduating, I joined the family business that my father ran in partnership with his brothers; I liked that job and dedicated myself enthusiastically to that world. I don't regret having made that decision and enjoyed my work; however, I tried to keep informed of the latest in scientific developments. I was greatly impressed by a book on astronomy that fell into my hands explaining the laws ruling the universe, with beautiful illustrations of the planets and galaxies. I wanted to learn everything possible about them and believe me; I read the book at least a hundred times. I was never able to explain why that subject fascinated me so. Why was I so impressed? I have no idea.

I wish you could help me out. What explanation can you give me? Why did you choose the priesthood? Definitely, I would never have thought to be a priest. It is not my calling, something that would give me satisfaction. I have no talent for that; I think I can be more useful where I am as it affords me the possibility of creating job opportunities. I can provide more benefits here than by preaching which doesn't fill the stomach of someone who is hungry.

But if forced to, I would choose to enter a monastery as a monk. At least my life would have meaning by belonging to a self-sufficient group founded with the purpose of serving and helping others. I would feel more useful. Or maybe as a missionary, but perhaps not, for I am embarrassed to confess that this calling is incompatible with my personality.

Friend Victor, I believe you haven't noticed that you could have offended me by what you just said. Why do you place the priesthood on a lesser level than that of a monk or a missionary?

My apologies if what I said offended you. I didn't mean to, for you well know that I have always admired your goodness and your dedication to helping others within your possibilities. It would be a gross error to generalize; it is true that we are made up of the good and bad, the skilled and clumsy, the sincere and hypocritical. I know you have the goodness and wisdom to recognize the good, and to ignore and forgive the bad.

But Victor, you have a way of thinking similar to mine.

Similar yes, but not the same. I cannot see myself preaching something as truth which is alien to my way of thinking.

REFLECTIONS OF A BELIEVER

But let's get back to the subject of the differences in abilities in man.

For goodness sake, Victor, it's obvious that you are setting me up!

Why would you think that? I'd like to know your opinion.

I really can't explain it; it's like knowing beforehand what direction you want to take in life.

I well know how you think, and that you are going to bring up the subject of reincarnation, which my religion rejects. I think that we live only one life, and after the body dies, we go on in mind and spirit to a different one, without having to return to occupy a body.

Forgive me Father Juan if I call your attention to what you have said is different from what your religion says, which assures us that at the end of time bodies will rise from the dead, whole in body and soul. Obviously, this is a concept I cannot accept for reasons already mentioned. But you said that your body dies once and your soul will not return to occupy another body. You are not being true to your religion.

What do you want from me? Why do you trouble me?

I don't wish to upset you, but would like that you not cling to your teachings and accept that there are different possibilities other than those taught by your religion. You should not believe undiscerning; you are an intelligent person with the right to question the commandments of men who claim to possess the absolute truth that should be blindly obeyed. Open your mind to other possibilities; analyze, seek YOUR truth without fear, a truth that could be different, but ultimately YOURS.

You have not given me your opinion about why you and I have different abilities, different talents.

For goodness sake, Victor, I don't know! Maybe by creating a soul to occupy a body, God is assigning it a mission, a specific talent to complement those of others.

That's your hypothesis, and we are unable to say yes or no regarding the matter. Nevertheless, a number of doubts occur to me.

Why eliminate the possibility that the mind and the soul existed from the beginning of time, before life itself developed?

Your religion states that the individual forges his eternal destiny in only one life. This is not the way I see it, but let's accept it that way.

Do you think it fair that this distribution of talents takes place as a gamble?

Let's just say that each soul gets to live just one life and that the most numerous cards are those that deal hardship and even hunger, and from this point on to the top of the pyramid, the good cards decrease exponentially on all levels of intelligence, health, capacity of achievement and success.

How many will suffer hunger, ignorance, illnesses, abuses, breaking their backs working from sunrise to sunset just to survive?

Climbing the pyramid improves the quality of life little by little until finally, on reaching the top, the fortunate ones will possess talent, creativity, power, and a comfortable lifestyle.

What bad luck of the one thousand million or more at the base of the pyramid? They have lived a miserable subhuman life of subsistence, suffering abuses, lack of hygiene, illnesses, and insults. They don't know that life should be a happy one and seek to escape it all by drowning themselves in alcohol.

What have they done to deserve that hell?

REFLECTIONS OF A BELIEVER

Victor, our religion tells us that they will inherit the kingdom of heaven.

Father Juan, my friend, if the souls of the poor and those who suffer, once their bodies have died, will have earned the kingdom of heaven - without taking into consideration that many of them could have been evil and cruel - don't you think it would be unfair to throw out what Christ tells us: You will be judged by your deeds? I think that this was contrived by men to cement the church's power and to keep the needy under control by offering them heaven for all eternity as a reward for being docile.

Where will the souls of those who have lived a more comfortable life go to?

Will those blessed by life with the opportunity for creating music, literature, scientific research, and wealth that allows a great part of humanity to live comfortably go to hell as punishment?

Wouldn't that be absurd? It would be like denying a fair and loving God.

You're right, it wouldn't be fair.

I believe that if there is a reward for each of us, poor or rich, ignorant or genius, it has to be based upon how near we come to love, human solidarity, aid to others, the capacity to forgive, compassion for the suffering. On the other hand, in no way do I believe in the hell described by Dante, which was in the best interests of the church; that is, to further tighten the yoke of terror on its believers.

I can't argue with what you have said, and believe there should be another more logical hypothesis. This subject is disturbing me. I cannot think of another option, even though I can see that my hypothesis has neither head nor tail. I confess that I have never meditated upon it, since it has been of unquestionable faith to me. I know that you are trying to corner me into considering reincarnation as a part of the divine plan. To even think of that possibility frightens me, for the church categorically denies it.

Did Christ deny it?

Not that I know of.

May I remind you that it was Justiniano, emperor of Byzantium and of the church who, in the sixth century, condemned the belief in reincarnation an autocrat who made that up on the spur of the moment, probably because it was an inconvenience to his interests?

What surprises me is that right in the twenty-first century the church still clings to nonsense that ultimately cannot be proven. But there have been many instances or people in deep hypnosis that described clearly previous lives.

I am convinced that reincarnation should be part of the divine plan. For me, it explains the apparent injustices of life; also the different level of intellectual evolution and the variety of talents and preferences present in all of humanity.

Thank you for your friendship; never once did I intend to offend you.

I know, and I thank you too – I shall meditate seriously on what we have talked about.

My respects, Father Juan. We are clearly in agreement on the basics: God, Jesus Christ, and that life of the Being continue after the death of the body. That is what bonds us, makes us brothers. The other concepts are not important. Our different ways of thinking about the unfathomable have never clouded our friendship.

CONCLUSION

I was born into a Christian family, nourished with love and tenderness, and the fundamental values were instilled in me by example to form the conduct of a lifetime: dignity, honesty, respect for my fellow man, fulfillment of my duty, responsibility, work, support of family, generosity, love of God, of Jesus Christ, of the Virgin Mary, and all that can enrich you spiritually.

I remember the peace, fraternity, and joy that invaded me at Christmastime: the *posadas*, the Christmas carols, the Christmas tree, and the Nativity scene.

Today, the tradition still continues but much of that fervor that inspired such a happy celebration has been lost. Why? It is evident that nowadays one lives a more hurried existence, more stressful and anxiety-ridden. Materialism consumes us and creates new needs; on not having access to them, we become depressed, and that affects our happiness. Unfortunately, an important number of young people, educated in this twenty first century, no longer find an answer to their spiritual concerns within the church. They question, and rightly so, the veracity of many concepts and beliefs that are given as truth, appropriate during the Middle Ages, but that today are untenable and fail a serious analysis.

It is also true that, although at a very slow pace, those erroneous concepts that awaken disbelief in others are being eliminated, and that is something very dangerous, for it could harm faith in the basic concepts that are, in my judgment, irrefutable truths. We should understand that the errors of the church are to be blamed exclusively on human beings; God or Christ have nothing to do with them.

It should be understood that we should modernize, that it is important to consolidate our faith basing ourselves only on the teachings of Jesus, on the Christian philosophy, on living His message as much as possible without deceit, concealment, or hypocrisy.

A religion without a church is better than a church without religion.

The church is not a religion; it is a powerful institution of human beings.

Religion is an idea, a concept born of the intuition of enlightened beings that provides, among other things, some important ethical rules for the coexistence of man, such as the tablets of the Law of Moses. Monotheism, the belief in one true God, Creator of heaven and earth, and the concept of life after death of the body, is another basic idea.

Jesus Christ, later on, enlightens us with His sermon based on the love of the Father, and He leaves us a religion based on love, of God above all, and of our neighbor. Love your neighbor, take pity on the fallen, feed the hungry, give drink to the thirsty, clothe the naked, be humble, be charitable; in brief, LOVE. He assures us of the immortality of the spirit, He astonishes us by His miracles, and at the end of His passage through life, and He gives us proof of His immortality. That is my truth, which is the religion He has bequeathed us.

The house of God is everywhere, not just in the enclosure of a parish or cathedral. A Christian church should adhere to the message, and understand that this is its true mission for, on the contrary, how can it represent Christ if His message is not honored?

What to do? It is clear: let us change direction by seeking the legitimacy of the church. How? By returning to the basics, eliminating the concepts that have been added over time by men who have clouded the true meaning of their pastoral mission and by concentrating on fulfilling the basic principles of the beautiful message left us by Jesus Christ.

MY TRUTH? GOD LOVES US, EXISTS AND ALWAYS HAS. CHRIST EXISTED BEFORE HIS LIFE ON EARTH, HE IS, AND WILL ALWAYS BE. HE IS AMONG US AND WILL ALWAYS BE. HIS MESSAGE WILL ENDURE FOREVER, IN SPITE OF THE ERRORS OF MANKIND.

www.ingramcontent.com/pod-product-compliance
Lightning Source LLC
Chambersburg PA
CBHW020007050426
42450CB00005B/358